T0328661

Cambridge Elements ≡

Elements in Ancient Philosophy
edited by
James Warren
University of Cambridge

STOIC EROS

Simon Shogry
Brasenose College, University of Oxford

Shaftesbury Road, Cambridge CB2 8EA, United Kingdom

One Liberty Plaza, 20th Floor, New York, NY 10006, USA

477 Williamstown Road, Port Melbourne, VIC 3207, Australia

314–321, 3rd Floor, Plot 3, Splendor Forum, Jasola District Centre,
New Delhi – 110025, India

103 Penang Road, #05–06/07, Visioncrest Commercial, Singapore 238467

Cambridge University Press is part of Cambridge University Press & Assessment,
a department of the University of Cambridge.

We share the University's mission to contribute to society through the pursuit of
education, learning and research at the highest international levels of excellence.

www.cambridge.org
Information on this title: www.cambridge.org/9781009500814

DOI: 10.1017/9781009039277

First published 2024

A catalogue record for this publication is available from the British Library.

ISBN 978-1-009-50081-4 Hardback
ISBN 978-1-009-01771-8 Paperback
ISSN 2631-4118 (online)
ISSN 2631-410X (print)

Stoic Eros

Elements in Ancient Philosophy

DOI: 10.1017/9781009039277
First published online: January 2024

Simon Shogry
Brasenose College, University of Oxford

Author for correspondence: Simon Shogry, Simon.Shogry@bnc.ox.ac.uk

Abstract: The Stoics distinguish two forms of eros. In vicious agents eros is indeed a passion and thus born out of a defective rational judgment about what is needed for happiness. But there is also a positive form of erotic love, practiced by the Sage on the basis of knowledge, which aims to reproduce his virtuous condition in others. In this Element, the author shows how the Stoics' wider theoretical commitments in ethics, epistemology, aesthetics, and psychology support their duplex account of eros. They also consider the influence of Plato's Symposium on the Stoic account, arguing for hitherto unrecognized links with Socratic moral psychology. The Element concludes with an assessment of how the Stoic erotic ideal fares in relation to our intuitions about the non-egoistic and particularized nature of love.

Keywords: Plato Symposium, Stoic love, Stoic emotion, Stoic moral psychology, erotic expertise

ISBNs: 9781009500814 (HB), 9781009017718 (PB), 9781009039277 (OC)
ISSNs: 2631-4118 (online), 2631-410X (print)

Contents

1 Introduction   1

2 The Two Basic Forms of *Erōs*   4

3 The Perception of Beauty   30

4 Socratic Antecedents for the Stoic Theory of *Erōs*   49

5 Conclusion   60

References   63

1 Introduction

"Stoic eros"? Isn't that a contradiction in terms? The ancient Stoics are notorious for their claim that the ideal human life is free of passion. So when it comes to arguably the most passionate emotion of all, we might expect them to take a uniformly dim view. Just like anger, fear, grief, and the other passions censured by Stoic theory, erotic love would seem to have no place in the best human life.[1]

Matters are not so simple, however. The Stoics identify an infamously erotic symposiast as their philosophical model – Socrates – and see themselves as working out with systematic rigor the theoretical outlook he introduced. For Socrates, *erōs* is by no means alien to the good life but rather intimately bound up with the acquisition of virtue and happiness. Underscoring this optimistic view, Socrates himself claims to possess erotic expertise (Plato, *Symposium*, 177d7–8; *Lysis*, 204b7–c2).

One goal of this Element is to show that the Stoics self-consciously embrace this Socratic precedent in formulating their account of *erōs*. Following Socrates, the Stoics make room in their ethical theory for a positive form of erotic love. The ideal human agent – the wise person or Sage, as the Stoics call her – is also a lover: her erotic expertise is an aspect of the knowledge in which the virtues consist, and her erotic efforts seek to improve the person whom she loves.[2] The Sage's *erōs* is not pathological, then, but a source of benefit and part of a happy, well-lived human life. But just as Socrates recognizes multiple expressions of *erōs*, only one of which reflects proper philosophical understanding and virtue, the Stoics distinguish a good form of erotic love, practiced by the Sage on the basis of her knowledge, from a blameworthy and passionate love that flows from ignorance. The result is a complex picture aiming to vindicate the Socratic insight that *erōs* can cooperate with virtue – and the powerful intuition that erotic love can be part of an objectively flourishing life – while also doing justice to the precarious and miserable nature of *erōs* grounded in vice.

Stoic philosophy is systematic, and so to better appreciate their account of erotic love – in particular, its duplex structure – we need to contextualize it within broader strands of Stoic thought. The Stoics posit virtue as the sole good and, as such, the one thing that genuinely benefits us and bestows happiness (*eudaimonia*); analogously, vice is the sole bad and, as such, the one thing that genuinely harms us and renders life miserable. Furthermore, the Stoics offer

---

[1] In what follows, I translate the Greek term *erōs* as "love" or "erotic love."

[2] As I discuss in Section 2.2, the Stoics maintain that "the virtue of men and women is the same" (DL 7.175), and they strenuously reject the idea that virtue is open to men alone. For this reason, I use both male and female pronouns to refer to the Sage.

a purely epistemic analysis of virtue and vice, according to which virtue consists in knowledge, and vice just is ignorance. The value of *erōs* for human beings thus depends on its relationship with these fundamental good and bad things – virtue and knowledge on the one hand and vice and ignorance on the other.

This relationship is the topic of Section 2. Here we will see that the Stoics distinguish the two basic forms of *erōs* according to the moral and epistemic condition of the lover. The Sage's *erōs* is good because it is inseparable from and guided by her virtue and knowledge, whereas vice and ignorance control the non-Sage's love (Section 2.1). The Stoics justify this account with their insistence that *erōs* is in every case a *rational* activity, in the sense that it is always a product of the lover's rational mind and responsive to her judgments about what is necessary for happiness. These value-judgments amount to ignorance in the non-Sage, since they are unstable and often false, but to knowledge in the Sage.

Here one might object that there is nothing rational about erotic love: surely it is rather a blind drive issuing from a part of us that lacks reason, floating free of our considered judgments about happiness and potentially opposing them. This intuition, however, is flatly denied by the Stoics. In general they reject the existence of non-rational parts of the soul, which motivate independently of the agent's cognition of the good, of the kind found in the tripartite theory of Plato's *Republic* and *Phaedrus*. Instead, adopting a position they consider originally Socratic, the Stoics defend a monistic psychological theory, on which the mature human mind is rational through and through. Consequently, every impulse for action is an expression of reason, according to the Stoics – reason perfected by virtue, in the case of the Sage, or reason corrupted by vice, in the case of the non-Sage.

This psychological theory has some surprising results. First, passions such as anger, fear, and grief spring from defective reasoning and rest on faulty cognition of what is good and bad for the agent. The same holds of the non-Sage's *erōs*, which the Stoics classify as a passion (Section 2.3). Second, the rational causes of our behavior are sometimes phenomenologically opaque to us: erotic love may present itself as an unbidden, inexplicable force, but in principle it can be traced back to the lover's views about the good (or so the Stoics argue). Third, there is no such thing as simultaneous mental conflict, that is, two impulses for contrary courses of action at the same time. Rather, as we will see in Section 2.3.1, when we consider Medea and Thrasonides – two ancient archetypes of conflicted lovers – the Stoics provide an alternative analysis.

If the Sage's *erōs* is not a passion, what is it? And how is it constitutively related to her knowledge and virtue? As we will see in Section 2.2, the Stoics define the Sage's love as "an effort to gain friendship." Such an effort is characteristic of the Sage, since to gain friendship (*philia*) with the beloved the Sage must reproduce her own knowledge and virtue in him.[3] This is because the Stoics restrict friendship to the wise, and the Sage's beloved is not yet in this perfected state. The Sage's *erōs* is thus essentially pedagogical – and asymmetrical in the moral and epistemic standing of the lover and beloved. The goal of wise love is to develop the talents of someone presently vicious to their full potential, so that he himself becomes happy, virtuous, and a friend to the Sage.

It is a commonplace in ancient thought that *erōs* is a response to beauty. The Sage's *erōs* is no exception, as it is more expansively defined as "an effort to gain friendship *resulting from the beauty that has been made to appear*" (emphasis added). Section 3 investigates what, exactly, the beauty of the Sage's beloved amounts to (Section 3.1), and how it is made to appear in the mind of the Sage (Section 3.2). I contend that this beauty is a feature of the beloved's soul, grounded in his heightened potential to become virtuous. This character trait – talent-beauty, as I will call it – is directly perceived by the Sage as a consequence of her possession of erotic expertise. In interpreting the Stoic theory this way, we can integrate their recognition of erotic expertise – on which the first two leaders of the school, Zeno and Cleanthes, each composed a full treatise – with their doctrine of "expert impressions." According to this doctrine, expertise enhances the precision and detail of the impressions (or appearances, *phantasiai*) the expert forms. So when faced with the same stimulus – for instance, a Beethoven symphony – the expert musician hears more in the piece than the amateur. Analogously, I suggest, features of character lost on the erotic amateur are made to appear in the mind of the Sage when a suitable beloved presents himself – including, crucially, his talent-beauty.

In Section 4, I examine the ways in which the Stoic theory of *erōs* can be understood as a response to, and development of, Socratic ideas on love as they are presented in Plato's *Symposium*. I contend that both Socrates and the Stoics understand *erōs* as a rational state, admitting of expertise, which motivates the lover to pursue what she takes to be good, beautiful, and productive of happiness (Section 4.1). For the Stoics, this Socratic insight offers the correct starting point for any satisfactory treatment of *erōs* and is seen as detachable from the metaphysics of Forms they regard as problematic. Here I depart from the scholarly consensus that identifies Pausanias, not Socrates, as the speaker in the *Symposium* who most directly influences the Stoic account (Section 4.2).

---

[3] As we will also see in Section 2.2, the Sage's love is neither hetero- nor homoerotic, and so in what follows I alternate between using male and female pronouns to refer to the Sage's beloved. Note that "friendship" will be my standard translation of *philia*, in contrast to "love" or "erotic love" for *erōs*.

This standard interpretation overlooks the deep theoretical affinities between Stoic and Socratic moral psychology and downplays the Stoics' principled criticism of traditional pederastic relationships, of the kind championed (with slight modifications) by Pausanias.

Finally, two remarks on the scope of my inquiry in this Element. First, I will say nothing about Stoic views on marriage, since the Stoics typically investigate the value and appropriateness of marriage on the assumption that spouses ought to feel goodwill and friendship for each other but not *erōs*.[4] Second, my discussion of sex will be limited to contexts where it is clearly related to *erōs* – for example, as the product of an erotic impulse (Sections 2.2.1, 2.3, 2.4). I therefore set aside questions about the role of sex within marriage and Stoic justifications for parenthood, since the Stoics tend to address these topics separately from their treatment of *erōs*. We must avoid the temptation, then, to construe the Stoic account of *erōs* as a general theory of sexuality – and still less as a general theory of interpersonal attraction and affection. In Section 5, I assess how the Stoic account of wise *erōs* fares in relation to our intuitions about the non-egoistic and particularized character of love, concluding that it preserves the former but struggles with the latter: although it is the beloved's good, not her own, that motivates the Sage to enter into an erotic relationship, we might worry that she places too little value on the concrete individuality of the beloved, above and beyond his possession of talent-beauty.

2 The Two Basic Forms of *Erōs*

In this section, I present the Stoic distinction between the two basic forms of *erōs*, one virtuous and the other vicious. At its worst, erotic love is a passion and so an erratic and disobedient impulse born out of unstable and false value-judgments. But at its best, erotic love is a beneficial activity that flows from the wise person's virtue and knowledge, helping the not yet wise beloved become good. The wise person will fall in love, the Stoics argue, but this virtuous form of *erōs* differs from the passionate and ignorant kind that afflicts the vicious. In Section 2.1, I lay out the ethical, psychological, and epistemological theses that lead the Stoics to draw this distinction. In Section 2.2, I consider the Sage's *erōs* in particular, which the Stoics define as "an effort to gain friendship," before examining in Section 2.2.1 whether sex has any role in this effort. In Section 2.3, I turn to the Stoic account of *vicious erōs*, contextualizing it within their more general theory of the passions; and in Section 2.3.1, I analyze the character of

---

[4] Musonius' claim to the contrary (fr. 14, 75.12–14, ed. Hense) is presented as exceptional and counterintuitive. See discussion in Reydams-Schils 2005, 145–59, and Gill 2013, 151–3. See also Epictetus' comments on the unusual marriage of Crates and Hipparchia (*Diss.* 3.22.76) and discussion in Inwood 1997, 68–9.

Thrasonides, the literary model used by the Stoics to illustrate how vicious lovers are capable of reform. Finally, in Section 2.4, I explain what unifies the two basic kinds of *erōs* and, with this account in hand, address some scholarly disputes concerning the different ways that *erōs* is characterized in our sources.

2.1 Virtue, Vice, and the Two Forms of *Erōs*

One central contention of this Element is that the Stoic account of *erōs* cannot be fully understood in isolation from the school's wider ethical, psychological, and epistemological theory. We thus find here a case study of the celebrated systematicity of Stoic philosophy. In this section, I show how Stoic thinking on virtue and vice supports their distinction between two forms of *erōs*.

One of our most informative reports on Stoic *erōs* is prefaced with the following remark:

> **T1**: And [the Stoics] say that the wise man does everything [he does] on the basis of all the virtues; for every action of his is perfect, and so is bereft of none of the virtues. (Stob. 2.65.12–14, Wachsmuth's text)

Before we discuss its relevance for the Stoic account of *erōs*, we should pause to notice how strong the claim in T1 is. It is not merely the claim of the "unity of the virtues," traditionally associated with Socrates in the *Protagoras*, that the agent who possesses one virtue (e.g. courage) necessarily possesses all the others too (e.g. prudence, justice, moderation). To be sure, the Stoics accept the unity of the virtues, on broadly Socratic grounds, since they hold that courage, prudence, justice, and moderation each consist in knowledge – and indeed in knowledge of the *same theorems* – so that one could not possess the knowledge that is courage without also possessing the knowledge that is prudence (or justice or moderation). For this reason, the Stoics say these virtues are "inseparable" from one another (Stob. 2.63.6–8) and "mutually imply" one another (DL 7.125).[5] However, the claim in T1 is that, each time the Sage acts, *all* the virtues are active. So in standing firm on the battlefield or distributing money to the needy, no less than in taking a walk after dinner, the Sage jointly exercises courage, justice, prudence, moderation, and all the other virtues too. No action of his is "bereft" of a single virtue.

This strong claim I will call the *cooperation of the virtues*, and, on the face of it, it seems quite implausible. Without further elucidation, it is hard to see how

---

[5] Strictly speaking, not all virtues consist in knowledge, but the non-epistemic virtues are said to "supervene" on the epistemic ones (Stob. 2.62.15–20) and hence will be inseparable from them (DL 7.90). Throughout this Element, I set aside this complication and use "virtue" to mean "virtue consisting in knowledge."

the knowledge that constitutes courage, for instance – the knowledge of "what is terrifying, not terrifying, and neither" (Stob. 2.59.10–11) pertaining to matters of endurance (Stob. 2.60.14) – could be active in the Sage's distributing money to the needy, or even in physical exercise. Why must *all* the virtues be active in such cases, rather than just one virtue or none at all?

T2 suggests one potential line of response. The Stoics, we learn, are committed to the unity and cooperation of the virtues, but they also maintain that the virtues

> T2: differ from one another in their main concerns (*kephalaia*). Prudence's main concerns are, in the first instance (*proēgoumenōs*), to theorize about and put into action what is to be done, but on the second level (*kata de ton deuteron logon*) to theorize also about what distributions one ought to make, what choices one ought to make, and what one ought to endure, for the sake of putting unerringly into action what is to be done. The special main concern of moderation is, in the first instance, to make one's impulses steady and to theorize about them, but on the second level to theorize about the matters that come under the other virtues, in order to conduct oneself unerringly in one's impulses. Similarly, courage theorizes in the first instance about everything one ought to endure, but at the second level about the matters that come under the others, and justice, in the first instance, investigates each person's due, but on the second level the remaining things too. For all the virtues look to the concerns of them all (*pasas gar tas aretas ta pasōn blepein*) and to the matters that are ranged under each other. (Stob. 2.63.10–25, trans. Cooper modified, Wachsmuth's text)

It is not immediately clear what it means for a single virtue (e.g. courage) to theorize about one group of theorems "in the first instance" (*proēgoumenōs*) and another group "on the second level" (*kata ... ton deuteron logon*). However, following recent scholarship, we can say that although all the virtues consist in knowledge of the same theorems, each virtue has its own "main concern" or special "perspective" on those theorems, such that it gives primary attention to a subset of them.[6] Thus courage differs from the other virtues in having a privileged theoretical awareness of "everything one ought to endure." But in order to comprehensively grasp these theorems related to endurance, courage cannot fail to "look to" the theorems given primary attention by the other virtues, and so it knows them too, albeit "on the second level." This is because, for the Stoics, neither the special perspective of justice, concerning "each person's due" and what should be distributed to whom, nor the main concerns of prudence, relating to "what is to be done," are ever fully separable from or

---

[6] See Cooper 1999, 96–104, Long and Sedley 1987, vol. 1, 384, and Schofield 1984, 93–4. Long and Sedley translate *kephalaia* in T2 as "perspectives," where Cooper gives "main concerns"; Schofield has "chief provinces."

irrelevant to determining which things ought to be endured and why. The principles of courage, which make *x* the thing to endure in a given scenario, are consistent with and informed by the principles of prudence, which make enduring *x* the thing to do, and so on with the other virtues: "the things to be done are also to be chosen, to be endured, to be held to, and to be distributed" (DL 7.126). It is impossible, then, that prudence would recommend φ-ing and courage not-φ-ing. Whoever acts on the basis of one virtue necessarily acts on the basis of them all, given how their main concerns are interrelated.

The Stoics defend the strong thesis of the cooperation of the virtues, then, because they think that each virtue contributes something from its primary area of concern to the production of each virtuous action. Thus Seneca speaks of the "inseparable entourage" (*individuus comitatus*) of the virtues and claims that every action performed by the Sage is "the work of one single virtue but arises out of the judgment of the whole council" (*una virtus facit, sed ex consilii sententia*: *Ep.* 67.10). So when the Sage donates money to the needy, she is acting justly, as she relies on her knowledge of "what distributions one ought to make" (e.g. that this kind of person should be helped before that person). But her just action in this case relies on the primary perspectives of all the other virtues as well: for instance, how to endure criticisms from others, should they arise, and so on. Indeed, the Stoics maintain that even something as humdrum as taking a walk after dinner, when performed by the Sage, reflects the global knowledge in which the virtues consist.[7] Why postprandial exercise is appropriate in this instance, in what way it should be performed, in preference to which other practical goals, etc., would be answered by the different virtues and their different perspectives on the common stock of theorems. The actions controlled and guided by the Sage's virtues are thus considerably wider in scope than those which philosophers today would classify as morally right or wrong.

But to what degree is the Sage aware of each of the individual virtues' epistemic contributions when she decides to act? In selecting the virtuous action, does she consciously attend to each virtue's perspective on why that action is correct? Or, rather, is at least part of the holistic knowledge in which the virtues consist latent and not consciously entertained? Since the subject matter of the virtues ranges widely, it seems the latter view is more charitable: consciously attending to the epistemic contributions of all the virtues at once would seem to require a superhuman feat of cognition, and the Sage is held out as a demanding, but still humanly attainable, ideal. Yet the Stoics also insist that the virtues are "always present" in the Sage "at every moment"

---

[7] Thus we find "prudent walking" (*phronimōs peripatein*) listed as one example of a virtuous action (*kathorthōma*) at Stob. 2.96.20–22. See also Seneca, *Ep.* 66.5, 36.

(Stob. 2.68.24–69.3; cf. DL 7.83), so that every action she performs is perfect, "containing all the right measures" (Stob. 2.93.14–16; Cicero, *Fin.* 3.24).

In my view, these commitments do not sit well with the possibility that any single virtue is fully latent in the psychological lead-up to a virtuous action. They point instead, I think, to an important Stoic principle about the workings of the rational mind that we will return to often in our discussion of *erōs*, which I will call the *opacity principle*.

> *Opacity Principle*: the cognitive causes of the rational mind's activities are sometimes phenomenologically opaque to the agent.

When applied to the cooperation of the virtues, the opacity principle allows the Stoics to say that, although every virtue is *causally active* in producing each virtuous action – and so no virtue is latent in this sense – some of the individual virtues' epistemic contributions may not be phenomenologically transparent to the virtuous agent at the time she acts, even if they are potentially recovered and made explicit later on. To be sure, the Sage has internalized the perspective of each virtue, and each virtue is causally active insofar as it leads the Sage – explicitly or implicitly – to select the virtuous action and to appreciate why it is correct. However, some cases may not require the Sage to consciously attend to (e.g.) the moderate dimensions of her just action, since the circumstances in which it is selected bring only justice's main concerns to the forefront of her attention.

This account of the psychology of virtue provides the context for the Stoic account of *erōs*, in particular for their claim that there is an *erotic virtue*. Immediately following on from T1, our source continues:

> T3: Consistently with this [i.e. with the claim in T1], they also hold that the one with intelligence (*ho noun echōn*)[8] acts in the manner of a dialectician, a symposiast, and a lover (*erōtikōs*). But "lover" (*erōtikos*) is said in two ways: one lover has this quality because of virtue, since he is excellent (*spoudaios*), whereas another lover gets this quality from vice, and is censured as a kind of erotic maniac (*erōtomanē tina*) ... They characterize the virtues exercised at a symposium similarly to those pertaining to love: the one being knowledge which is concerned with what is appropriate at a symposium, namely, of how one should run symposia and how one should drink at them; and the other [sc. erotic virtue] is knowledge of how to hunt for talented young people, which turns them to virtue – and in general knowledge of loving well. That is why they say that the intelligent person will be a lover. (Stob. 2.65.15–66.9, trans. Inwood and Gerson modified)

---

[8] Accepting Mullach's emendation. I otherwise read Wachsmuth's text of T3.

T3 seeks to justify the Stoic thesis that the Sage (the "intelligent" or "excellent" person) engages in *erōs*, in a way that is consistent with the Stoic commitment to the unity and cooperation of the virtues in T1.[9] The strategy is to posit an erotic virtue. This implies that there is a specifically erotic perspective on the theorems known in common by the other virtues. Although the special perspective or concern of erotic virtue is not identified here, as it is for courage, moderation, and so on in T2, we may infer that erotic virtue theorizes in the first instance about how to help talented young people become virtuous, as this is the knowledge it is associated with in T3.[10] The Stoics are therefore proposing that in order to effectively theorize about this topic – and more generally about "loving well" – erotic virtue must "look to" the main concerns of the other virtues, from which it is inseparable.

This account of erotic virtue is highly abstract. Even so, it enables us to draw some preliminary conclusions about the Sage's erotic activities, which will be corroborated in more detail as we go on. First, the Sage's *erōs* will be sensitive to and flow from the comprehensive knowledge in which the virtues consist, with the result that wise love will operate under certain constraints: it will never be unjust to the beloved or to anyone else, never impious, cowardly, or hubristic. Second, the Sage's *erōs* has a pedagogical aim: to make the talented beloved virtuous. Third, given the cooperation of the virtues, erotic virtue will make an epistemic contribution to all the Sage's actions, so that he will never miss out on an opportunity to develop the talents of a young person and turn them to virtue, should he meet with someone who would stand to benefit from his erotic efforts. Fourth, in circumstances where erotic matters are especially salient to the Sage – for instance, in the ancient context, a symposium – erotic virtue will cooperate with other virtues in accomplishing its pedagogical goal. So if the Sage encounters a talented youth at a symposium, his sympotic virtue, for example, will cause him not to drink so much that it becomes impossible to help the youth become virtuous.[11] Moreover, in such a scenario, the Sage will

---

[9] The author of T1–T3 regularly refers to the Sage, or virtuous person, as "excellent" (*spoudaios*): see, for example, Stob. 2.99.3–8, a Stoic usage that may go back to Zeno. Similarly, "intelligence" (*nounecheia*) names an aspect of the knowledge in which prudence consists (Stob. 2.61.4), and so presumably the "intelligent person" (*ho noun echōn*) will be the person in possession of such knowledge, that is, the Sage. On the "talented young people" mentioned in T3, see Section 3.

[10] See also Seneca *Ep.* 81.12: "only the Sage knows how to love." I provide further specification of the Sage's erotic knowledge in Section 3.2.2, when I turn to the Stoic account of erotic expertise. I then compare Stoic and Socratic erotic expertise in Section 4.2.

[11] The Sage will drink wine but never to the point of getting drunk (DL 7.118; cf. 7.127). See Schofield 1991, 41–2. The Stoic Diogenes also connects erotic and sympotic virtue, insofar as they have similar goals – friendship and cheerfulness, respectively (Philodemus, *On Music* IV col. 47, lines 11–22) – and because they have a special connection with musical melodies (ibid., col. 43, lines 37–45). See also Philo, *SVF* 3.301.

also deploy the dialectical virtues to avoid assenting to any falsehood, should one happen to be blurted out by a fellow symposiast in his cups.[12] Finally, in T3's grouping of erotic, sympotic, and dialectical virtue – used here as an illustration of the unity and cooperation of the virtues, in place of the quartet found in T2 (viz., prudence, moderation, courage, and justice) – one suspects a special purpose: perhaps it alludes to the figure of Socrates and his famous blend of excellent erotic, sympotic, and dialectical activity.[13]

Before developing these points further, we should note that T3 also anticipates central features of the Stoic account of *vicious erōs*, that is, of the erotic activities performed by imperfect agents who lack virtue and knowledge.

By the Stoics' own admission, the Sage is exceedingly rare, and what disqualifies the vast majority of human beings from possessing knowledge and virtue is the overall instability of their belief set.[14] On the one hand, ordinary agents tend to hold false opinions, for example in ethics, about what is good and bad, about what contributes to or detracts from happiness. On the other hand, even when the non-Sage forms true judgments, his commitment to these truths is shaky and insecure, since in some circumstance or other he could be moved to abandon them.[15] This is because the non-Sage lacks the systematic understanding that characterizes the Sage's attachment to the truth. The Sage fully appreciates *why* the true judgments she holds are true – she is able to trace their explanatory relations to other truths and identify their place in the overall nexus of theorems – and so no amount of cajoling or persuasion could lead her to revise her commitment to them: hence, her true judgments amount to knowledge, each being "a grasp that is secure and unchangeable by reason" (Stob. 2.73.19–21). By contrast, the judgments of the non-Sage count as ignorance, "for ignorance is a changeable and weak assent" (Stob. 2.111.20–1).

Notice the modal language in the Stoic account of ignorance: if a judgment is change*able* in some case or other, then it counts as ignorance. So even when a judgment never actually gets changed, nonetheless, if it could be, for example in response to the pressures of contrary argumentation or temptation, then the agent is ignorant of it and does not know it. The Stoic claim, then, is that since everyone but the Sage could be moved to give up at least one of their judgments under certain circumstances, no one but the Sage has any knowledge of any truth, and in the absence of knowledge there is no virtue. For this reason, the

---

[12] According to the Stoics, "dialectic itself is necessary, and a virtue which includes others as species; non-precipitancy is knowledge of when one should and should not assent" (DL 7.46).

[13] Thanks to David Sedley for this suggestion.

[14] As Frede 1999, 295–6, has shown, this thesis also has a Socratic pedigree.

[15] This also applies to the non-Sage's "grasps" (*katalēpseis*), that is, his acts of assent to impressions whose causal history ensures they could not be false. For further discussion of grasps in Stoic epistemology and, in particular, of the insecure grasps of the non-Sage, see Shogry 2022.

Stoics deny that there are degrees of knowledge or ignorance, and hence also that there are degrees of virtue or vice: just as a stick is either straight or not straight, so too one's judgments are either potentially changed by rational means or they are not.[16] So, returning to T3, whenever a non-Sage enters into an erotic relationship, he does so under the influence of ignorance: vice endows his *erōs* with a blameworthy quality and reveals him as "a kind of erotic maniac" (*erōtomanē tina*).[17]

This latter description recalls the more general Stoic doctrine that every non-Sage, that is, every vicious and ignorant person, is insane.

> **T4**: When the Stoics say that all who are not Sages are insane, it is as though they were saying that all mud stinks. "But it doesn't always stink", you say. Stir it with a stick; you'll smell it. (Cicero, *Tusc.* 4.54, trans. Brennan)

Even though the ordinary lover may appear calm and content now, his erotic attachment rests on an underlying unstable cognitive disposition, a counterfactual susceptibility to give up not only the particular judgments he has made about the beloved but also his more general ethical views about what will bring him happiness. Ignorant lovers, the Stoic Chrysippus observes, tend to reject advice against gratifying their *erōs*, and they persist in their erotic relationships even after publicly declaring that doing so is not to their own advantage (Galen, *PHP* 4.6.27–30). We have to treat these lovers, Chrysippus says, like those who "have lost their senses" and "are at variance with themselves ... neither acting like themselves nor in possession of their faculties."[18] The later Stoic Panaetius also emphasizes the volatility of vicious *erōs*, warning those "who are a long way from Sagehood" to avoid "something which is turbulent, out of control, forsworn to someone else and cheapened in its own eyes" (Seneca, *Ep.* 116.5). Chrysippus and Panaetius converge, then, in criticizing the erotic activities of the non-Sage on the grounds that they involve changing evaluative judgments on the part of the lover. At the root of the vicious agent's erotic endeavors are ignorance and insanity, even if this debilitating psychological condition is sometimes opaque to and unrecognizable by the lover herself.

---

[16] The stick analogy appears in Simplicius, *Cat.* 8.237–8 and DL 7.127. The Stoics use further analogies to the same effect: just as one is either above the water's surface or below it, or blind or not blind, so too one is either virtuous and knowledgeable or vicious and ignorant (Plutarch, *Com. Not.* 1063a–b; Cicero, *Fin.* 3.48, 4.64). The rejection of degrees of virtue and vice is also reflected in the Stoic claim that all moral errors are equal, since "they all derive from vice as from a single source" (Stob. 2.106.21–3; cf. DL 7.120, Cicero, *Stoic Paradoxes* III.20–6).

[17] Here the Stoics reject rival philosophical theories, as well as a central strand of Greek popular thought, linking erotic mania with a *positive* form of love: see Section 4.

[18] Galen, *PHP* 4.6.24 (trans. after De Lacy): ὡς περὶ ἐξεστηκότων ... καὶ ὡς πρὸς παρηλλαχότας ... καὶ οὐ παρ' ἑαυτοῖς οὐδ' ἐν αὑτοῖς ὄντας. See Inwood 1997, 64–8, and Tieleman 2003, 170–8. See also Cicero, *Tusc.* 4.76.

Certainly for some modern readers, and the Stoics' ancient critics too, it is difficult to conceive of a praiseworthy form of love that is entirely without inconsistency or mania.[19] We might think that insanity is built into *erōs*: without some degree of transience and irrationality, a state may be virtuous and admirable but not any recognizable form of erotic love. The Stoics disagree. When integrated into the perfected mind of the Sage and guided by the knowledge in which the virtues consist, love is neither flighty nor excessive but instead a stable source of benefit. It remains to be seen, of course, how the Stoics go about filling in this sketch. But it should now be clear that the wider commitments of Stoic moral psychology and epistemology lead them to distinguish two basic forms of *erōs*: one virtuous and based on knowledge, the other vicious and ignorant. Because an agent's *erōs* is qualified by his vice, if he is vicious, or by his virtue, if he is a Sage, the term "lover" is not univocal (T3).

2.2 The Sage's *Erōs*

A relatively uniform definition of the Sage's *erōs* emerges from a series of reliable reports:

> **T5**: They say that love is an effort to gain friendship resulting from the beauty belonging to young people in their prime that has been made to appear; and that is why the wise person is a lover and will love those who are worthy of love, as they are well-born and talented. (Stob. 2.115.1–4)

> **T6**: And the wise man will love young people who create an impression, through their form, of a talent for virtue, as Zeno says in the *Republic* and Chrysippus in book one of *On Ways of Life* and Apollodorus in his *Ethics*. And love is an effort to gain friendship resulting from the beauty that has been made to appear; and it is not directed at intercourse, but at friendship. (DL 7.129–130)

> **T7**: Love is an appetite for bodily intercourse. . . . Another love is a service to the gods through the correct ordering of the young and beautiful, which they call an effort to gain friendship resulting from the beauty that has been made to appear. (Ps.-Andronicus, *On Passions* 4 = *SVF* 3.397)

> **T8**: But these men's loves [sc. those of famous Greek pederasts] are all of the appetitive kind. We philosophers have arisen, on the authority of our Plato himself . . . to give official sanction to love. Indeed, the Stoics say that the wise person will fall in love. They give as their definition of love "an effort to form a friendship, due to an impression of beauty". If such a love exists in the world – one without worry, without need, without care, without sighing – then

---

[19] See Inwood 1997, 68–9, and Nussbaum 1998, 294–8. For ancient criticism along these lines, see Plutarch, *Com. Not.* 1073c and Cicero, *Tusc.* 4.71–2 (T8 below, on which see Graver 2002, 179).

so be it. For that love is free from all appetite. (Cicero, *Tusc.* 4.71–2, trans. Graver modified)

T6's definition of love as "an effort to gain friendship resulting from the beauty that has been made to appear" (*epibolēn philopoiias dia kallos emphainomenon*) nicely encapsulates the cognate accounts of the Sage's *erōs* given above in T5–T8, the group of texts I will henceforth refer to as our *core sources*. In this section I will explicate the initial elements of this definition by explaining what it means for virtuous love to be an "effort"; why it aims at friendship; and how it is related to piety and divine service (T7). I postpone until Section 3 consideration of "the beauty that has been made to appear" (*kallos emphainomenon*: T5–T7) – or, equivalently, "the impression of beauty" (*pulchritudinis species*: T8) – which is said to spark wise *erōs*.

First, what is meant in describing the Sage's love as an "effort" (*epibolē*: T5–T7; *conatus*: T8)? This term has a specialized use in Stoic psychology, where it names a particular kind of impulse: "an effort is an impulse before an impulse" (*hormēn pro hormēs*: Stob. 2.87.18). Although this remark is not further explained, it suggests that each effort is a complex impulse, one comprising further token impulses in an arrangement of temporal or logical priority.[20] So if one forms an effort to φ, one thereby also takes on a commitment to perform a series of further actions (ψ_1, ψ_2, ...) in a determinate order, which together have φ as their overarching goal. Supporting evidence for this reconstruction is found in Epictetus, who praises a student's effort to live according to Stoic principles, which is said to consist in the study first of physics and then of theology (*Diss.* 1.12.7–8). Similarly, Chrysippus remarks that the Academic skeptic undertakes to argue both for and against any thesis put to him, on the grounds that, through such actions, he will achieve his effort to induce universal suspension of judgment (Plutarch, *St. Rep.* 1035f–1036a).

So construed, "effort" would be an apt description of the Sage's *erōs*, whose overarching goal is the creation of friendship (*philopoiia*: T5–T8). To become friends with the beloved, a *series* of actions must be performed, one after another. The Sage's love should therefore be understood as a long-term enterprise, an effort encompassing a number of further impulses that together aim at making the beloved a friend.

Now, given Stoic assumptions about the nature of friendship, in seeking to become friends with the beloved, the wise lover is thereby also seeking to improve him and make him virtuous. This is because only the wise are friends, according to the Stoics (DL 7.124; Stob. 2.108.15–25), and, unlike the Sage

---

[20] Thus Inwood 1985, 232–3; Schofield 1991, 29n14; Price 2002, 184n24.

herself, her beloved is not yet wise. The ultimate purpose of the Sage's erotic effort is therefore to reproduce her own condition of virtue in the beloved and turn him into a friend. For this reason, the Stoics identify friendship as the goal (*telos*) of love (Philodemus, *On Music* IV, col. 47, lines 11–22) and classify as one type of friendship "erotic friendship, created out of *erōs*" (Stob. 2.74.9–10).

The pedagogical aim of wise love is consistent with the Stoic claim that virtue is teachable (DL 7.91) and helps to fill in our picture of the Sage's more general protreptic mission.[21] The Sage knows that virtue is necessary and sufficient for human happiness and is motivated by this knowledge to make the beloved happy *through* making them virtuous. We will return in Sections 4.2 and 5 to assess the philosophical plausibility of the Stoic claim that the ideal erotic relationship is essentially pedagogical and thus asymmetrical in the moral and epistemic standing of the lover and beloved. We may observe now, however, that the Stoic theory can at least respect the intuition that a good lover helps their beloved realize their potential and become the best version of themselves. Such a goal could never be accomplished by securing the beloved a certain job or promotion or any other external reward, the Stoics think, as these outcomes are not really good for their possessor. Rather, the sole good is virtue, and so to genuinely benefit the person she loves and make them happy, the Sage must help them acquire virtue. It is toward this goal, therefore – and with it friendship – that the Sage's erotic effort is ultimately directed.

That the Sage's love is educational in purpose and aims at the inculcation of virtue and friendship in the beloved is now the consensus view among interpreters.[22] Three implications of this doctrine are worthy of further comment here.

First, wise love could never arise between two Sages, since the beloved in this case would be already virtuous and thus stand in need of no further moral improvement.[23]

---

[21] See Stob. 2.104.14–6: the Sage has been turned to virtue and turns others to virtue as well; Stob. 2.105.1–2: only the Sage is capable of turning others to virtue; Stob. 2.108.5–7: the Sage is "affable in conversation and charming and capable of turning others [sc. to virtue] and capable of hunting for (*thēreutikon*) good will and friendship through his conversation." On the parallels between Stob. 2.108.5–7 and T3, see Schofield 1991, 29n13. James Warren reminds me that, according to one common usage in DL, to be "hunted" (*thērathēnai*) is to become the pupil of an established philosopher and take up the philosophical life (e.g. Crantor being "hunted" by Polemo at DL 4.17).

[22] On the pedagogical aim of wise love, see the pathbreaking remarks by Schofield 1991, 32–5, who is followed by Inwood 1997, 59–60, Nussbaum 1998, 291–3, Price 2002, 187–8, Graver 2007, 188–9, Gill 2013, 145, and Collette-Dučić 2014, 88–9. The precise role of wise love in Stoic political philosophy, beyond its use in propagating virtue and friendship in the ideal state of Zeno's *Republic*, remains controversial: see Athenaeus, 13.561c, and discussion in Schofield 1991, 35–56, Boys-Stones 1998, and Vogt 2008, 154–60.

[23] *Pace* Gaca 2000, 212. DL 7.131 does not claim that Sages feel *erōs* toward each other.

Second, since the Stoics emphatically reject the notion that virtue is open to males alone – Cleanthes devoted an entire book to arguing that the virtue of men and women is the same (DL 7.175; cf. Plato, *Meno* 71e–73c) – it follows that there can be wise lovers of both sexes. Both men and women could possess the knowledge of how to turn talented young people to virtue (T3) and be guided by it when such a person presents themselves. I say "themselves" here, since talent, too – the quality of the beloved toward which the Sage's erotic effort responds (T5–T6) – is present in men and women alike (Plutarch, *Amat.* 767b), and so the ideal beloved need not be male, contrary to what we might expect from the norms of Greek pederasty and from ancient reports on Zeno's own sexual proclivities (Athenaeus, 13.563d–e).[24] Wise love is therefore neither hetero- nor homoerotic, on the Stoic view, since one's sexual organs make no difference to virtue – either to the possession of it now or to the propensity to acquire it later – and so to one's status as a wise lover or a talented beloved.[25]

Third, if we accept the reliability of T7, the Sage's erotic effort is also understood as an expression of piety, insofar as it is "a service to the gods through the correct ordering (*katakosmēsis*) of the young and beautiful."[26] From one perspective, the piety of the Sage's *erōs* is unsurprising, since the wise person is said to be pious and god-loved (Stob. 2.100.4). Moreover, the Stoics claim that "the gods find virtue and its deeds congenial" (Stob. 2.105.25–6) and regard the Sage's erotic effort as one such virtuous deed (T3). Indeed, since every virtuous action is done on the basis of all the virtues, there is a sense in which *all* virtuous actions express piety and have an equal claim to be congenial to the gods. T7, however, suggests a specific rationale for the piety of the Sage's *erōs*: it is a service to the gods *through* the correct ordering of the young and

---

[24] We may recall that Plato famously investigates the comparative talent (*euphuia*) of men and women for the philosophical way of life in *Republic* 5 (see especially 455b4–c3).

[25] Here I agree with Schofield 1991, 43–6; Inwood 1997, 59; Nussbaum 1998, 291; Price 2002, 186; and Bett 2010, 147. See also Lactantius, *Div. Inst.* 3.25, who reports that the Stoics encouraged women to study philosophy. Plutarch, *Amat.* 767b (cited in the main text) claims it would be "absurd" to deny that talent is found in both sexes: this could be read as an objection posed by Plutarch to any Stoic who argued to the contrary, but given the well-attested Stoic commitment to the irrelevance of biological sex for the possession of virtue I am inclined to take it instead as an implication the Stoics would accept.

[26] Von Arnim excises the quoted words of T7 from *SVF* 3.397, and he is followed by Gilbert-Thirry 1977, 28, and Schofield 1991, 30n17, who supposes that the author of T7 has here interpolated Polemo's definition of love as "a service to the gods through the care and salvation of the young" (Plutarch, *To an Uneducated Ruler* 780d). However, the formulation given in T7 differs from Polemo's, and the remainder of the report, containing the definition of wise love appearing throughout the core sources, is surely Stoic. Furthermore, the piety of the Sage's love is testified independently by Cicero (*Fin.* 3.68), and the Stoics elsewhere define the virtue of piety as "knowledge of service to the gods" (DL 7.119; Stob. 2.62.2–3, 68.7). I thus see no reason to regard T7 as untrustworthy.

beautiful, that is, *through* making them virtuous.[27] The language here of "service" (*hupēresia*) recalls a stretch of argument in Plato's *Euthyphro*, where Socrates and Euthyphro puzzle over which goal our service to the gods could help achieve, on the assumption that piety is a kind of human service to the gods (13d8–e14). Euthyphro cannot ascertain what this goal could be, but perhaps the Stoics take up this question in their account of the pedagogical character of wise love: the Sage serves the gods through her erotic efforts by bringing into the world more pious and god-loved beings, that is, more virtuous agents – the beautiful young people who have been "correctly ordered" and made virtuous through their contact with the Sage.[28] There is good reason, then, to take the Stoic spokesman of Cicero's *De Finibus* at face value when he describes wise love in pious terms, as something "sanctified" (*sanctus*: 3.68).

2.2.1 Sex and Wise Love

In turning the beloved to virtue, the Sage's erotic effort constitutes a service to the gods, but could this holy vocation ever involve sex? Obviously, sex is not the *goal* of wise love, as it is for the appetitive form of love marked off in T6 and T7 (see Section 2.3). But one might suppose that the Sage's pedagogical objectives rule out any kind of physical intimacy with the beloved.[29] Certainly, to convey the theorems of dialectic or physics, for instance – knowledge of which is inseparable from, and an aspect of, the global knowledge that constitutes the virtues (DL 7.46–7, 83, 92) – sex would be an entirely inappropriate tactic.[30] We can safely assume, then, that, in comparison with vicious appetitive love, sex will occupy a much diminished place within the Sage's erotic effort. Given the serious business of imparting systematic philosophical knowledge – without which there is neither virtue nor friendship nor happiness – the default encounter between wise lover and talented beloved must surely be nonsexual. The Stoics encourage such a view with their claim that what makes someone worthy of the Sage's love is not to be "worthy of being sexually enjoyed" (*axiapolaustos*) but rather to be "worthy of friendship" (*axiophilētos*: T14, discussed in Section 3.1.2). It is the educable condition of the beloved's soul – a heightened psychological potential to acquire the knowledge in which the virtues consist

---

[27] The virtuous agent is elsewhere described as orderly (Stob. 2.115.12–14; cf. DL 7.126; Stob. 2.60.20–1).

[28] Taylor 1982, 111–12, argues that this kind of view is in fact Socrates' own in the *Euthyphro*.

[29] Compare Srinivasan 2020, who convincingly argues that sex, transpiring in the present-day university context between professors and their students, is to be prohibited on the grounds that it constitutes "a pedagogical failure."

[30] For some sense of the – decidedly nonsexual – pedagogical methods standardly employed by the Stoics to inculcate knowledge, see, for example, Plutarch *St. Rep.* 1035f–1036a, with discussion in Shogry 2022, and Seneca, *Ep.* 87, with discussion in Shogry, in press.

and become the Sage's friend – that incites and sustains the erotic attraction of the wise.

However, we cannot overlook the Stoics' principled opposition to imposing categorical prohibitions on any given action-type, including, presumably, sex. Early Stoic treatises on ethics and political theory, much maligned by a hostile ancient tradition that formed around them, defend a series of "disturbing theses," as Katja Vogt calls them, regarding the permissibility of such practices as cannibalism and incest. However, as Vogt and others have shown, far from recommending these shocking practices as general policy, the Stoic founders instead argue that they are appropriate only in extreme circumstances.[31] Incest, for instance, is justified in the hypothetical scenario where a father and daughter are the last two humans alive (Origen, *SVF* 3.743), and cannibalism is defensible in situations like the Donner Party's (cf. Sextus Empiricus, *PH* 3.347). These commitments point to a powerful strand of ethical particularism in Stoic theory and a clear rejection of exceptionless rules forbidding a given action-type, since in bizarre or desperate circumstances even the most ingrained taboos could have a reasonable defense and be appropriate to perform.[32] Given this theoretical outlook, it would be highly surprising for the Stoics to deny that sex is sometimes justified in the context of an erotic relationship between the Sage and her beloved. The Stoic view would then be that, although sex is not ordinarily the appropriate way of inculcating knowledge and virtue, it could be in some conceivable scenario, and so wise love is not necessarily ascetic.[33]

2.3 Vicious *Erōs* and the Stoic Theory of the Passions

It is now time to examine in more detail the erotic activities of ordinary agents. How exactly do the Stoics characterize vicious *erōs*, in contrast to wise love? In Section 2.1, we saw that every non-Sage enters into an erotic relationship under the influence of ignorance and insanity, in the sense that all such relationships rest on an insecure cognitive foundation: the vicious lover's opinions about what her own happiness requires, and about the beloved's contribution to it, are subject to change, often in unpredictable and irrational ways. In this section, I will show that the psychological volatility characteristic of vicious *erōs* is also reflected in T8's suggestion that the non-Sage's love is "of an appetitive kind"

---

[31] See Visnjic 2021, 39–42; Vogt 2008, 20–64; Schofield 1991, 5–14.

[32] Thus Gill 2013, 155–6. On ethical particularism, see Dancy 2017. Recall here one Stoic definition of "appropriate action": "that which, when done, admits of a reasonable defense" (DL 7.107). In ordinary cases, cannibalism and incest have no reasonable defense: it is only in dire straits that they are justified.

[33] Zeno emphasizes that, in these cases, the appropriateness of sexual intercourse does not depend on the gender of the beloved (Sextus Empiricus, *PH* 3.245).

(*lubidinosus*) and in T7's account of *erōs* as an "appetite" (*epithumia*). This will involve contextualizing vicious *erōs* within the more general Stoic theory of the passions (*pathē*), as the Stoics use "appetite" to pick out one of the four main types of passion (DL 7.110; Stob. 2.88.14–15).

As alluded to in the Introduction, the Stoics maintain that the virtuous agent suffers no passions (*pathē*) and hence that the best human life is passion-free (*apathēs*) (DL 7.117). Only the vicious are afflicted by passion, the Stoics think, since every passion is an "impulse which is excessive and disobedient to the dictates of reason, or a movement of soul which is irrational and contrary to nature" (Stob. 2.88.8–10; cf. DL 7.110), whereas the Sage always acts in perfect agreement with nature (DL 7.87–9).

Notice, first, that the Stoics define the passions as impulses of a certain kind. This implies that all passions are created through the exercise of the vicious agent's mind, since every impulse arises from the mind's assent to an action-guiding impression (Stob. 2.86.17–87.5). The Stoics confirm this implication with their claim that "all passions belong to the ruling part of the soul" (Stob. 2.88.10), since in mature human beings "the ruling part of the soul" is just another name for "the mind" (Stob. 2.65.1–3), which is rational through and through. Passions are therefore "irrational" and "disobedient to the dictates of reason" not because they have a non-rational source; the Stoic claim is rather that to suffer a passion is to use one's reason *badly*.

We can make this claim more precise by noting that, for the Stoics, to undergo a passion is to judge incorrectly and disobey *right* reason, that is, the rationality of the cosmos or Zeus or nature as a whole – the god's-eye perspective on what is genuinely good and bad for the agent and productive of her flourishing. In support of this contention, the Stoics adopt a cognitivist analysis of the passions. Each passion, they hold, can be accurately described as an opinion (Galen, *PHP* 4.2.1), a judgment (DL 7.111), or a "weak supposition" (Stob. 2.88.22–89.2), whose content includes two elements, both of which (in the standard case) are false: (i) an ascription of value to an object that is present or in prospect and (ii) an assessment that a particular course of action is appropriate to perform in response.[34]

In standard cases, (i) is false because the passionate agent mistakes something he currently possesses or expects to possess as either good or bad, when really it is indifferent. So, for instance, the passionate delight that Mr. Burns

---

[34] See Klein 2021, 236–42, Graver 2007, chap. 2; Brennan 2005, chap. 7; Nussbaum 1994, chap. 10; Inwood 1985, chap. 5. Recall also that ignorance is defined as "weak assent" (Stob. 2.111.20–1), underscoring the connection between passion and ignorance. Similarly, the Stoics describe each passion as a "fluttering" (*ptoia*) (Stob. 2.88.11–12) and characterize the insanity that afflicts the non-Sage as "fluttery ignorance" (*agnoia ptoiōdēs*) (Stob. 2.68.22–3).

takes in his massive accumulation of wealth consists, in part, in his mind's assent to the proposition that wealth is something good – where "good" carries the eudaimonist connotation of being conducive to his happiness (cf. Stob. 2.90.9; Seneca, *Ep.* 59.14–15). This judgment is false, the Stoics maintain, since the presence of wealth makes no difference to one's happiness. This case of passion, then, involves a cognitive failure: in feeling delight, Mr. Burns has incorrectly evaluated wealth and misjudged its connection to his own flourishing.

Moreover, in undergoing this passion, Mr. Burns may also experience pleasant uplifting sensations and an internal effervescence – what the Stoics call an "expansion" or "swelling" of the soul – as a result of his judgment that such actions are appropriate responses to his possession of wealth (element (ii) above). On the Stoic view, this assessment is also false, for these are not objectively appropriate reactions to the presence of something that is not authentically good.[35]

As mentioned, the Stoics recognize four main types or genera of passion. Each genus is distinguished by the character of its intentional object: (1) distress, a present perceived bad; (2) fear, a future perceived bad; (3) delight, a present perceived good; and (4) appetite, a future perceived good. What is common in all four genera, however, is the two-element cognitivist analysis given above and an error of judgment on the part of the agent regarding these two elements, that is, an epistemic failure incompatible with virtue. This is one upshot of Chrysippus' runner analogy (in Galen, *PHP* 4.2.10–18). Just as a runner moves in such a way that he is "carried away" and cannot immediately come to a halt, so the passionate agent acts on impulses "going beyond the rational proportion", that is, contrary to right reason.

However, some commentators see the runner analogy as gesturing at a sense in which, for Chrysippus, the passionate agent disobeys their *own reason* as well.[36] Passions can thus be understood as out-of-control, recalcitrant impulses whose psychological inertia leads the agent to disregard the practical priorities they have previously formed (cf. Stob. 2.89.4–14). According to Chrysippus, Menelaus' *erōs* for Helen nicely illustrates this runaway character of the passions. Menelaus creates an impulse to kill Helen but abandons it when "struck by her beauty" and kisses her instead (Galen, *PHP* 4.6.9). On Chrysippus' account, Menelaus' erotic appetite is strong enough to dislodge the practical judgment he earlier reached while more or less clearheaded and

---

[35] For a general explanation of why element (ii) is false, and of nonstandard cases in which element (i) is true, see Graver 2007, chap. 9. Compare Brennan 2005, 96n11.

[36] See Graver 2007, 68: in a state of passion, Chrysippus suggests, "it is as if the rational mind has lost the ability to execute its own commands." See also Tieleman 2003, 170–8.

deliberating over what would best advance his own interests. The important point here is not the particular judgment that Menelaus arrived at through deliberation – Chrysippus is not endorsing the propriety of murder! – but rather its susceptibility to being overturned by his subsequently formed erotic appetite.

With this context in view, we can now better appreciate what is at stake in classifying vicious *erōs* as a passion and, more specifically, as an appetite (T7–T8). According to the cognitivist analysis we have just presented, appetite is a disobedient impulse created by the vicious agent's assent to a proposition combining two elements: (i) a false ascription of goodness to an object in prospect and (ii) a judgment about which action(s) would be appropriate to perform in response to that object. Furthermore, T7 identifies the non-Sage's *erōs* as "an appetite for bodily intercourse." I thus see two broad strategies for filling out the false composite judgment in which the non-Sage's erotic appetite consists. I sketch both strategies here to indicate how the Stoics could have further specified appetitive *erōs* into its various forms, depending on the case in question.[37]

First, bodily intercourse might be the prospective object envisioned as good in (i), so that vicious *erōs* would rest on the opinion that (i) sex with the beloved is good, and (ii) it is appropriate for me to φ_1, φ_2, ... The φ's here stand in for the various token actions performed by the agent with a view to wooing the beloved and attaining the putative good that is the sexual conquest. Vicious *erōs* would thus have a similar complexity as the Sage's erotic effort but would be directed at the wrong goal – sexual activity disconnected from the virtuous psychological disposition of the Sage is not good (see T12 in Section 2.4) – and would be pursued in a way that overrides the lover's previously established practical objectives. So construed, vicious *erōs* would be closely related to the appetite the Stoics call "salaciousness" (*lagneia*), or "the excessive appetite for intercourse" (Ps.-Andronicus, *On Passions* 4).

Second, T7 could be specifying the behavioral component of vicious *erōs* (bodily intercourse) but not the prospective perceived good toward which it is a response. On this construal, different vicious lovers could hold different opinions about which feature of their beloved is good, that is, conducive to their happiness – his looks, his wealth, his power, his sense of humor, his sexual prowess, or even just his continued existence and presence in the lover's life – which would in turn imply their commitment to different views about why sex

---

[37] In my view, there is likely no *single* Stoic formula for fixing the propositional content of the erotic appetite in every case. The Stoics show a keen interest in taxonomizing the subspecies of the passions within a larger genus, as we can gather from surviving lists detailing the varieties of appetite, delight, fear, and distress (e.g. DL 7.110–4; Stob. 2.90–2; Ps.-Andronicus, *On Passions* 1–5). See Graver 2007, 55–8.

with the beloved is appropriate. Of course, the ordinary lover may not ever make such opinions explicit to herself in carrying out her relationship with the beloved, but, given the opacity principle (Section 2.1), the Stoics need not assume she will: the point is that such opinions are causally active in leading the agent to love whom she does, whether or not she consciously attends to them.

According to this second strategy, then, element (i) of the opinion on which vicious love rests might differ across vicious agents, even though element (ii) – the judgment that sex with the beloved is appropriate – remains the same. This would require the Stoics to offer different explanations of the falsity of the composite judgment, depending on the case in question, but their general strategy here must be twofold. First, they would insist that the shapeliness of the beloved's body, his external possessions, and any character traits he has that are divorced from virtue are *neither good nor bad* and thus not a true source of happiness for the lover. Second, they would deny that the putative but inauthentic goodness of the beloved justifies sex with him at any cost. There are often other important values at stake that make intercourse inappropriate – a fact that would be obvious to the lover were they not in passion's grip. This latter point comes into sharper focus upon considering the Stoic reaction to the case of Thrasonides.

2.3.1 Thrasonides' Erōs

The Stoics, Chrysippus especially, look to poetry for corroboration of their ethical and psychological theory. Euripides is frequently cited for this purpose, as we saw just now with Chrysippus' invocation of Menelaus' erotic appetite for Helen (Galen, *PHP* 4.6.9; cf. Euripides, *Andromache* 629–30), as is Homer. Stoic moral psychology is therefore presented as a theory that "fits the data" of ordinary experience, as dramatized by the poets, despite the paradoxical air of many Stoic doctrines.[38] It is in this spirit, I submit, that Chrysippus appeals to the action of one of Menander's plays – *The Hated Man*, popular in antiquity but now surviving only in fragments – as an illustration not only of the appetitive nature of vicious *erōs* but also of how non-Sages ought to respond to this passion and begin to ameliorate their erotic mania. Moreover, the same play is cited by Epictetus in one of his discourses on vicious *erōs*, suggesting that within the Stoic school *The Hated Man* enjoyed pride of place as the standard cultural reference point for their account of appetitive love.[39]

Following on directly from T6, we read that

---

[38] As Nussbaum stresses (1994, 368–9).

[39] Previous studies make only passing reference to Stoic interest in *The Hated Man*: see Gill 2013, 145, Gaca 2000, 230n68, Nussbaum 1998, 292, and Inwood 1997, 59.

T9: Thrasonides, then, although he had his beloved in his power, kept his hands off her because she hated him. So love is directed at friendship, as Chrysippus says in his *On Love*. (DL 7.130)

Thrasonides, a successful soldier back home from fighting, is the titular character of *The Hated Man*, whose plot revolves around his relationship with the young Krateia, his beloved, for whom he has a "most manic love" (*emmanestata erōs*: 11–12).[40] Krateia has come into Thrasonides' possession as a prisoner of war and now lives in his home. Legally, then, she is "in his power" (T9), having been established as a mistress (37–40). Krateia, for her part, has conceived an "unholy hatred" (43) of Thrasonides and spurns all his advances. Thrasonides feels confused and dejected – "have you ever seen a more miserable man," he asks in the opening soliloquy, "or one with worse fates in love?" (4–5) – but nonetheless keeps his distance from Krateia, pacing outside his home while she stews indoors. Other characters in the play admire Krateia's qualities, praising, in particular, her self-knowledge (*oide ta heautēs polu*: 534–6). Later on, having been rejected by Krateia once more, Thrasonides declares his friendship (*philia*) for her and states that his life would not be worth living without her (708–11); then, chastising himself for thinking only of himself and not Krateia, he attempts suicide (799–816). What happens next is uncertain, owing to the poor state of the text, but it is clear that the suicide is foiled and, moreover, that Krateia eventually becomes reconciled to Thrasonides and agrees to marry him.

Refraining to rape one's slave is hardly the mark of a moral saint, but Thrasonides is not held out by the Stoics as a Sage. For Epictetus, Thrasonides' erratic behavior over the course of the play reveals his "slavery" to Krateia and the manic proclivity of all impassioned agents to give up their previously held ethical opinions (*Diss.* 4.1.19–23). By contrast, T9 suggests that Chrysippus' interest in Thrasonides' *erōs* lies rather in its utility in showing how even vicious agents can come to appreciate the value of friendship and, on this basis, check their violent and aggressive appetitive love.[41]

Consistent with their theory of the passions, Stoic exegesis of *The Hated Man* could begin with the observation that Thrasonides' *erōs* for Krateia is bound up

---

[40] For a new edition of the text of the play, together with an English translation and notes, see Furley 2021. All my citations to line numbers of the play are to this edition, and I largely follow Furley's translation.

[41] Given the sorry state of our evidence, it would be rash to conclude that Epictetus' uniformly critical remarks constitute a rejection of Chrysippus' approach to *The Hated Man*. In his *On Love*, Chrysippus may have put forward similar criticisms as we find in Epictetus, while also going on to explain Thrasonides' potential for moral improvement. More generally, Stephens contends that Epictetus "stands . . . against the Greeks of the early Stoa" in "condemning all *erōs* as objectionable *pathos*" (1996, 194). However, as Stephens himself notes (1996, 197), Epictetus does once speak of *erōs* as "in a way divine" (*Diss.* 4.1.147).

with the opinion that he cannot be happy without her. The prospect of being permanently despised by and separated from Krateia moves him to attempt suicide (799–816), and, earlier in the play, when asking Krateia's father for permission to marry her, Thrasonides describes the answer to his request as determining whether he will be "either happy or the most miserable person of anyone alive" (660–3: *ē makarion ē trisathliōtaton . . . tōn zōntōn hapantōn*). Thrasonides' erotic impulse thus rests on the judgment that Krateia's presence is *good* for him in the full-blown eudaimonist sense of making his life go well, just as we would expect from the cognitivist analysis of the passions the Stoics endorse (specifically, element (i) of the second analysis of appetitive love given in Section 2.3).

The mental conflict Thrasonides experiences is also amenable to Stoic analysis. Undoubtedly, Thrasonides sometimes feels *erōs* for Krateia: he confides to the audience that he desires to do to Krateia what any ordinary lover does to their beloved, "but I do not" (11–12). How would the Stoics explain Thrasonides' ability to curb his erotic impulse for sex and pursue a contrary course of action? As we have seen, the Stoics deny that the erotic impulse originates in a non-rational part of the soul: it is instead a product of reason. So, since reason cannot simultaneously form two conflicting impulses – since it cannot affirm, at one and the same time, that (e.g.) sexual intercourse is both appropriate and not appropriate to do – mental conflict is instead characterized as an oscillation, over time, between these impulses (Plutarch, *Mor. Vir.* 446f–447a).[42] Such conflict may be *felt* as simultaneous – in line with the opacity principle (Section 2.1), its diachronic character need not be phenomenologically transparent to the agent – but it is always a shift in the judgment of reason as a whole, at successive points of time, that is its cause. So, as Krateia is locked up in his house, Thrasonides undergoes a rapid fluctuation between an erotic impulse for sex and a contrary impulse to refrain, with the latter ultimately winning out.

Thrasonides' case of mental conflict offers an instructive contrast with that of Euripides' Medea, which also elicited Chrysippean commentary.[43] Spurned by her lover Jason, Medea is torn between vengeance and compassion. On the Stoic analysis, her impulse to spare her children contends against – but after a period of oscillation finally loses out to – her passionate impulse to murder them. By contrast, Thrasonides gives up his violent

---

[42] Thus Gill 2006, 221–3, Brennan 1998, 28–9, Long and Sedley 1987, vol. 1, 422, and Inwood 1985, 137–9.

[43] Specifically, Euripides, *Medea* 1078–9. Chrysippus' interest in these lines is reported by Galen at *PHP* 4.6.19–20. See also Epictetus, *Diss.* 1.28.7–9. For discussion, see Graver 2007, 70–2, Gill 2006, 258–60, and Tieleman 2003, 171–3. For a Chrysippean reading of Seneca's *Medea*, see Nussbaum 1994, 448–53.

Table 1 Two cases of mental conflict

	Non-passionate impulse	Passionate impulse
Medea	To spare her children.	*To murder her children.*
Thrasonides	*To refrain from sex with Krateia.*	To force himself on Krateia.

passion and refrains from forcing himself upon Krateia. We can thus compare these two cases of mental conflict in Table 1 (with italics indicating the impulse that wins out in each agent).

Using non-Stoic terminology, we can call Thrasonides continent or self-controlled, insofar as his mental conflict is resolved by abandoning his aggressive passion, and Medea incontinent or weak-willed, since she follows through on her murderous anger despite having deliberated on the more peaceable alternative.[44]

On what grounds does Thrasonides abandon his appetitive *erōs*? More specifically, what kind of *rational* consideration leads him to decide that sex with Krateia is inappropriate? Here again a Chrysippean explanation could be supplied. Consider this report on a disagreement between Chrysippus and Cleanthes on how best to console an agent suffering from grief (a form of distress):

> **T10**: Some hold that the comforter has only one responsibility: to teach the sufferer [sc. of grief] that what happened is not anything bad at all. This is the view of Cleanthes … . Chrysippus, for his part, holds that the key to consolation is to get rid of the person's opinion that mourning is something he ought to do, something just and appropriate. (Cicero, *Tusc.* 3.76, trans. Graver modified)

In the context of his account of the therapy of grief, Chrysippus proposes to remove element (ii) of the composite judgment in which this passion consists, the opinion that certain forms of behavior – outward displays of mourning such as weeping in public or beating one's breast – are appropriate to perform. In putting forward this strategy of consolation, Chrysippus reportedly diverges from Cleanthes, who suggests instead to target element (i) of the grieving agent's composite judgment, that the death of the person being mourned is genuinely bad. Cicero, our source for T10, later confirms that both these strategies are understood as generally applicable to all types of passion, not

---

[44] The Stoics do not follow Aristotle in distinguishing continence (*enkrateia*) from virtue and incontinence (*akrasia*) from vice. See Inwood 1985, 136–7. For a parallel case to Thrasonides' – of continence, roughly speaking – appearing in classical poetry and cited by Chrysippus, see Galen, *PHP* 3.3.2–3 (Odysseus beating his breast and not taking revenge on the suitors, at Homer, *Od.* 20.14–21) and discussion in Graver 2007, 71–2.

just grief (*Tusc.* 4.60), and so it is perhaps unsurprising to find Chrysippus writing elsewhere that:

> T11: Even if pleasure were the good, and supposing that the person mastered by passion takes this view, nevertheless one ought to help him and indicate to him that every passion involves an inconsistency, even for those who maintain that pleasure is the good, i.e. the goal. (Origen, *Contra Celsum* 8.51.30–3, trans. Chadwick modified)

Here Chrysippus envisions a case where a vicious agent "mastered by passion" holds the false opinion that "pleasure is the good, i.e. the goal." This surely corresponds to element (i) of the composite judgment in which his passion consists, as it is a false opinion concerning the agent's happiness, i.e. the goal of life: bodily pleasure is indifferent, not good, on the Stoic view (DL 7.102). As we saw in T10, Chrysippus, unlike Cleanthes, proposes to leave this opinion unchallenged, at least provisionally for immediate consolatory purposes, and instead to target element (ii), the appropriateness judgment. So it seems that in T11 Chrysippus is suggesting that one should "help" the impassioned agent by "indicating" that element (ii), the appropriateness judgment, "involves an inconsistency" with some other element of the agent's belief-set, perhaps even with element (i) itself.[45]

Of course, in Thrasonides' case, we are not dealing with an impassioned agent who is committed to a hedonist type-(i) judgment, that is, to the false opinion that pleasure is the sole good. Rather, as we concluded, element (i) of Thrasonides' erotic appetite attributes goodness to Krateia's friendship and presence in his life – a judgment, we may note, that he never abandons at any point in the play. So then, perhaps Chrysippus supposes that Thrasonides discards the type-(ii) judgment, that it is appropriate to have sex with Krateia, on the basis of detecting its inconsistency with his type-(i) eudaimonistic judgment: forcing himself upon her would thwart any hope of befriending her and spending their lives together, the prospective good on which he takes his happiness to depend.

If this is right, then Thrasonides represents a promising kind of non-Sage whose commitment to the value of making friends with the beloved is secure enough to get him to renounce any hubristic erotic activity incompatible with this goal. So, even though Thrasonides fails to practice *erōs* in the manner of the Sage – and surely has not yet come to appreciate all that friendship requires, according to the Stoic account – he is still on the right path in his views about the connection between love and friendship (at least *de dicto*). Chrysippus could fairly argue that, at some level of abstraction, Thrasonides correctly sees the

---

[45] The interpretation given here of T10 and T11 follows Graver 2007, 196–201.

force of the Stoic doctrine that "love is directed at friendship" (T9). To be sure, further work is needed to reform and stabilize Thrasonides' belief set as a whole. Nonetheless, we may conveniently term Thrasonides a "progressor lover" to distinguish him from other vicious agents further behind in moral progress (*prokopē*) whose erotic mania remains untreated.[46] Compared to these agents, including those whom Chrysippus calls "women-mad" (*gunaikoma-neis*) on account of their entrenched psychological disease (Galen, *PHP* 4.5.19–23; Athenaeus, 11.464d), Thrasonides has made a start in reforming himself and has learned how to resist appetitive love when it threatens friendship.[47] The Thrasonides case, then, as dramatized by Menander and interpreted by Chrysippus, contains a kernel of truth about the nature of wise *erōs* and portrays an imperfect agent progressing toward it.

2.4 The Unity of *Erōs*

Now that we have distinguished the two basic forms of *erōs* in Stoic theory, one virtuous and the other vicious, it is time to consider what, if anything, *unifies* them. "Lover" is said in two ways (T3), but to what extent are virtuous and vicious *erōs* structurally similar? Our discussion so far points to three shared features.

First, all forms of *erōs* share the same psychological genus, each being an *impulse* of a certain kind: virtuous *erōs* is defined as an effort, or an "impulse before an impulse" (Section 2.2), whereas vicious *erōs* is an appetite, one type of passion and, as such, an "impulse which is excessive and disobedient to the dictates of reason" (Section 2.3). Impulse is the psychological event respon-sible for action, and, as we have seen, the actions brought about through erotic impulses include pursuits of external objectives (e.g. sex with the beloved) as well as internal phenomenological feelings (e.g. a sense of elation and uplift when one's overtures are accepted). As we will see momentarily, the Stoics in T12 use the term "love-activity" (*to eran*) as a catch-all label for these external and internal activities brought about through erotic impulses.

---

[46] Although all moral errors are equal, and vice, ignorance, and unhappiness do not come in degrees (see Section 2.1), the Stoics distinguish vicious agents according to how much moral progress they have made, that is, according to how closer or farther from attaining virtue they are. This claim is incorporated into the image of the drowning man, who can be closer or farther from the surface of the sea (i.e. from virtue): see Plutarch, *Com. Not.* 1063a–b; Cicero, *Fin.* 3.48, 4.64.

[47] On psychological diseases in Stoicism and their role in stimulating passion, see DL 7.115, Stob. 2.93.1–13, Cicero, *Tusc.* 4.23–33, and discussion in Shogry 2021. Psychological diseases are distributed unevenly among vicious agents (only some people are irascible or women-mad, for instance).

This allows us to identify a second feature common to all cases of *erōs*: emotional engagement. In the case of ordinary love, this feature is obvious, as the non-Sage's appetitive *erōs* is a form of passion. However, as several commentators have plausibly suggested, the Stoics must have classified the Sage's erotic effort as a kind of *eupatheia* and so literally as a "good feeling."[48] In general, the Stoics distinguish the good feelings (*eupatheiai*) of the Sage from the passions (*pathē*) of the non-Sage, on the grounds that the former rest on a correct understanding of what is objectively beneficial or harmful for the agent.[49] So while the Sage suffers no passions, she nevertheless feels "joy" (*chara*) in the present goods she enjoys – for example, in her present condition of virtue and its expression in virtuous activity – and has a "wish" (*boulēsis*) for future goods, where both of these good feelings are rooted in knowledge and accompanied by a positive phenomenological valence. So, in helping the talented beloved progress toward virtue, the wise lover lacks the volatility, self-deception, and excessiveness characteristic of appetitive *erōs* but, for all that, is not emotionally inert during this process. As a good feeling, the Sage's erotic effort is phenomenologically rich.

Third, and crucial for my account of the Socratic antecedents of Stoic theory (Section 4), *erōs* is always guided by a form of evaluative cognition – a *rational* assessment by the agent concerning what is needed for happiness, often false in the case of the non-Sage but amounting to knowledge in the Sage. Of course, given the opacity principle (Section 2.1), the lover may not have consciously attended to endorsing any such eudaimonistic claim in the lead-up to their erotic activities. But nonetheless, on the Stoic view, *erōs* necessarily follows upon and is caused by a judgment about what the lover's personal flourishing requires, including the beloved's role in it. Thus the base vicious lover falsely predicates goodness to sexual intercourse or to some feature of the beloved that is divorced from virtue (Section 2.3), whereas the Sage's knowledge of the goodness of virtue and of how to reproduce it in the talented people she meets (T3) motivates her to make the beloved happy *through* making them virtuous (Section 2.2). Thrasonides, as a progressor lover, is not yet free of mental conflict and vacillates in his ethical judgments and impulses but ultimately resists appetitive *erōs* on the strength of his rational commitment to the value of friendship (Section 2.3.1). In all these cases, then, the Stoics posit a tight link between

---

[48] Thus Gill 2013, 148–9, Graver 2007, 187–9, Price 2002, 190, and Inwood 1997, 60n14, although no text explicitly confirms this suggestion.

[49] DL 7.116; Ps.-Andronicus, *On Passions* 6; Cicero, *Tusc.* 4.12–14. For general discussion of the *eupatheiai* and their phenomenological manifestations, see, for example, Graver 2007, 51–3; Cooper 2005; Brennan 2005, 97–8.

the character of the agent's erotic impulse and the overall condition of their rational mind, including the content of their eudaimonistic judgments.

I will now conclude Section 2 by raising some objections to my reconstruction of the two basic forms of *erōs* in Stoic theory.

One influential study has proposed that, for the Stoics, *erōs* is *never* a passion (Schofield 1991, 29–31, 112–14). This claim faces the difficulty of explaining away Chrysippus' and Panaetius' verbatim remarks to the contrary (Section 2.1) and is obviously in tension with my account of appetitive *erōs* (Section 2.3). Nonetheless, one text might seem to support this reading (T12 below), and its proponent argues that if *erōs* were counted among the passions, then the Stoics "could hardly have allowed that the Sage will love."[50]

However, the duality of *erōs* prevents this inference from going through. The Sage can love, provided that wise *erōs* is distinguished from other forms of *erōs*, found exclusively in the non-Sage, which count as passions: since the Sage never performs the latter, he remains passion-free. This is why the Stoics are at pains to emphasize that "lover" is said in two ways (T3). Indeed, one can find other examples of the Stoics using the same term in two ways, to mark out both a praiseworthy action and a blameworthy passion: "rivalry," for instance.[51] And it is standard Stoic doctrine that the Sage and non-Sage perform the same external action-types for different reasons and on different psychological grounds: this is one of the basic contrasts between merely appropriate actions (*kathēkonta*) and fully virtuous actions (*kathorthōmata*).[52] These points help to contextualize the Stoic insistence in the continuation of T3 that

> T12: Love-activity just by itself (*to eran auto monon*) is indifferent (*adiaphoron*), since at times it also occurs among the base. But love (*erōs*) is not an appetite nor is it directed at any base object, but is an effort to gain friendship resulting from the impression of beauty. (Stob. 2.66.9–13)

The first sentence of T12 confirms that it is not only Sages who engage in *erōs*: "the base", that is, non-Sages, do so also. More precisely, both virtuous and

---

[50] Schofield 1991, 29. More precisely, Schofield claims that *Zeno* does not include *erōs* as a passion, and that later Stoics "presumably due ultimately to Zeno's influence" follow him in denying that *erōs* is a passion (30n17). However, as we have already seen, Chrysippus posits an appetitive form of *erōs* (Galen, *PHP* 4.6.27–30) and generally does not flinch from defending the doctrines laid down in Zeno's *Republic* (as Schofield 1991, 26n10, demonstrates), where the Zenonian material on *erōs* would have been found. I thus find it unlikely that Zeno was the sole Stoic scholarch to deny the existence of passionate *erōs*.

[51] See Cicero, *Tusc.* 4.16 on *aemulatio*. Cf. Stob. 2.92.7–10 and Ps.-Andronicus, *On Passions* 2 (= *SVF* 3.414) on *zēlos*. Recall that wise *erōs* is denied to be "blameworthy" (*epimemptos*) at DL 7.130 (reading Dorandi's text).

[52] See Stob. 2.85.13–86.4 and 2.96.18–97.5; Cicero, *Fin.* 3.58–9; Sextus Empiricus, *M.* 11.200–1.

vicious agents form impulses directed at "love-activity" (*to eran*).[53] For this reason, love-activity is said to be "indifferent": considered "just by itself", that is, in abstraction from any token erotic impulses formed in particular circumstances by particular agents, love-activity is neither good nor bad, just like walking or speaking – action-types that other Stoic texts call "intermediate" (*mesa*), in the sense that they can be selected by both Sage and non-Sage – and unlike action-types that imply either moral success (e.g. doing justice) or moral failure (e.g. doing injustice).[54] In other words, T12 denies that love-activity just by itself is the exclusive province of either Sage or non-Sage: without knowing who carried out such activity, for what reason, and in what way, we are not in a position to determine whether it is praiseworthy or blameworthy, virtuous or vicious (as we would be able to do if we knew, e.g., that someone were doing injustice). I thus understand "love-activity" (*to eran*) in T12 as a broad category, picking out whatever types of outward and inward behavior are produced in common by both virtuous and vicious erotic impulses, including sex and positive phenomenological feelings.[55]

The second sentence of T12, by contrast, seems to corroborate the contention that *erōs* is never passionate, for it flatly denies that *erōs* is an appetite. Note, however, that this sentence opposes love's being an appetite with love's being "an effort to gain friendship resulting from the impression of beauty" (the "effort definition," as I will call it). The clear implication is that any kind of *erōs* that satisfies the effort definition is not an appetite (see also T8). So, if it could be shown that the Stoics' effort definition of *erōs* picks out wise love *only*, and not the *erōs* of the non-Sage, then T12 would not rule out the existence of appetitive love: rather, it would serve to clarify that the Sage's erotic effort does not count as an appetite, while leaving open the possibility that other forms of *erōs* do, on account of failing to meet the effort definition. Going forward, then, we will need to determine how widely the effort definition of *erōs* is meant to apply: to all forms of *erōs*, or instead (as I have claimed so far) to wise love in particular?

Some scholars have taken the effort definition as universally applicable, that is, suitable to characterize the erotic activities of both Sage and non-Sage.[56]

---

[53] The Stoics typically use verbal infinitives (e.g. *to peripatein*, *to dialegesthai*) to express predicates (*katēgorēmata*), and they identify these action-predicates as the objects of impulses. See Stob. 2.88.2–6 and Cicero, *Tusc.* 4.21, together with Bobzien and Shogry 2020, 4–7.

[54] See Stob. 2.85.13–86.4 and 2.96.18–97.5.

[55] Inwood and Gerson's translation of *to eran* in T12 as "sexual activity" (1997, 207) is thus too narrow. Outward action-types such as striking up a conversation, not to mention internal phenomenological responses, could also be included among the objects of virtuous and vicious erotic impulses. On sex and wise love, see Section 2.2.1.

[56] Bett 2010, 143, Laurand 2007, 71–3, and Schofield 1991, 112–14. By contrast, I share the assessment of Graver 2007, 185–6, Price 2002, 183–4, and Nussbaum 1998, 290, that the effort definition applies only to wise love.

In favor of this suggestion is perhaps the intuitive idea that all agents, regardless of their moral standing, respond to beauty with *erōs*. Since the effort definition identifies "the impression of beauty" as the initial cause of *erōs*, it would seem to respect this intuition. However, as we will see in Section 3, when we examine the role of beauty in the effort definition and consider the varieties of beauty recognized by the Stoics, it is possible to respect this intuition without taking the effort definition to capture the erotic activities of the non-Sage. Furthermore, applying the effort definition to vicious *erōs* has serious interpretative costs.

On the one hand, there is an unmistakable tendency in the core sources (T5–T8) to associate the effort definition with wise love in particular. Indeed, T5 infers from the effort definition that the Sage will love, and T7 explicitly contrasts appetitive *erōs* with the *erōs* picked out by the effort definition, which in turn is characterized as an expression of piety, a virtue found only in the Sage. Moreover, Plutarch concedes to the Stoics that, in hunting for talented youths and seeking to become friends with them, the Sage is not acting passionately (*Com. Not.* 1073c), and Alexander of Aphrodisias thinks the Stoics' effort definition picks out a kind of love that is "civilized" (*asteios*: *SVF* 3.722). On the other hand, the effort definition serves poorly as an account of vicious *erōs* in general, since many cases of appetitive love do not aim at the creation of friendship, even *de dicto*. Non-Sages more often seek from their erotic engagements sex, power, or some goal other than friendship: Thrasonides' hard-won insight that *erōs* and friendship are constitutively related is what earns him special praise. So if we insist on shoehorning all forms of vicious *erōs* into the effort definition, we obliterate the category of the progressor lover and saddle the Stoics with an implausible account of the psychology of ordinary agents, for whom the creation of friendship often plays no role – either explicitly or implicitly – in motivating their erotic activities. On balance, then, it seems best to interpret the effort definition as an account of wise love in particular and to understand the erotic activities of vicious agents as forms of appetite.[57]

3 The Perception of Beauty

The Sage's choice of beloved is far from artless, and she does not expend her erotic efforts on just anyone. Rather, she judges correctly that an erotic relationship is an appropriate response to a particular kind of person, someone

---

[57] In two obviously confused texts (DL 7.113 and Stob. 2.91.15–6), *erōs* is both listed as an appetite and defined as an "effort to gain friendship, resulting from the beauty which has been made to appear," which implies that the Sage never engages in the form of *erōs* captured by the effort definition, a result that makes nonsense of our core sources. This mangled report is thus of no help to those who construe the effort definition as universally applicable.

well-positioned to benefit from her attention and become good. In Section 3.1, I examine the various erotic qualities attributed to the Sage's beloved, arguing that they all refer to his psychological aptitude for virtue: the beauty such a person displays, then, differs both from conventional physical beauty and from the kind of beauty that, on the Stoic account, is coextensive with goodness and found in the Sage alone. In Section 3.2, I propose that the beloved's propensity for virtue is a character trait that is directly perceptible by the Sage – not inferred – as a result of her possession of *erotic expertise*. Such expertise is a crucial aspect of the knowledge linked to erotic virtue in T3, as it enables the Sage to perceptually detect who would be a suitable beneficiary of wise *erōs*.

3.1 The Erotic Qualities of the Sage's Beloved

That the Sage's beloved is prone to acquire virtue, but lacks it at present, emerges from the various ways they are characterized in our sources. They are said to be talented (*euphuēs*: T3, T5, T6), worthy of love (*axierastos*: T5, T14, and T15 below), well-born (*eugenēs*: T5), beautiful (*kallos/pulcher*: T5–T8), in their prime (*hōraios*: T5), and possessing the ripeness for virtue (*anthos aretēs*: T6). My contention in this section is that all these descriptions pick out a *single condition* of the Sage's beloved, namely their propensity for virtue – a psychological character that is readily improved and made good. Here, then, we find the Stoics challenging customary views of culturally salient erotic qualities: the beautiful, well-born beloved – the person *genuinely* worthy of love – is the person with the promise for virtue, not necessarily the bombshell with the dazzling body. The Stoics are engaged in a similar effort with their famous declarations that "only the Sage is free," "only the Sage is rich," and other such "Stoic Paradoxes."[58] Here, however, the revisionary project is extended to the Sage's *beloved*, who is not yet virtuous, and to the beauty, good-birth, and other erotic qualities they are said to exhibit. Moreover, youth is prized in the Sage's beloved (T5–T7; cf. Sextus Empiricus, *M.* 7.239) because it implies malleability of character, not (e.g.) a smooth and supple body: "for," as Seneca explains, "the young and talented are most easily made to become lovers of what is honorable and correct" (*Ep.* 108.12). To better understand her educable but not yet virtuous condition, let us examine the various descriptions applied to the Sage's beloved. I begin with the erotic qualities indisputably grounded in and referring to her potential for virtue – talent and

---

[58] See, for example, Cicero, *Stoic Paradoxes* V–VI, Stob. 2.67.13–68.17, and discussion in Vogt 2008, 126–30.

good-birth – before defending my more controversial claim that, likewise, her beauty consists in this same feature.

3.1.1 Talent and Good-Birth

Talent and good-birth are preferred indifferents (Stob. 2.81.1, DL 7.106) and thus object-types whose possession does not require virtue: just as one can be healthy or famous without being virtuous, so too can non-Sages be talented and well-born. Furthermore, the talent of the Sage's beloved is explicitly connected with the aptitude for virtue – it is said to be a "talent *for virtue*" (*euphuia pros aretēn*: T6, Plutarch, *Amat.* 767b) – and the same holds of her good-birth, as we learn from a debate transpiring between two sets of Stoic theorists:

> **T13**: As for talent and good-birth, some members of the school were led to say that every Sage is endowed with these attributes; but others were not. For some think that one is not only endowed with a talent for virtue by nature, but also that some are such by training ... And they took a similar view about good-birth, so that generally talent is a condition congenial to virtue which comes from nature or training, or a condition by which certain people are prone to acquire virtue readily, and good-birth is a condition congenial to virtue which comes from birth or training. (Stob. 2.107.14–108.4, trans. Inwood-Gerson modified)

All parties to this intra-Stoic debate agree that both talent and good-birth are psychological conditions "congenial to virtue," that is, congenial to its acquisition.[59] Rather, their disagreement concerns how these conditions are first acquired – by nature or training – and consequently whether all Sages possess them.

We can understand the contours of this debate as follows. On the one hand, if talent and good-birth are acquired solely by nature – if one's proclivity to become virtuous depends only on one's dispensations from birth and the natural course of one's development into adulthood[60] – then a Stoic theorist could be led to deny that all Sages are endowed with these attributes: some Sages could manage to acquire virtue despite lacking a natural propensity for it. In the background here is surely *Meno*'s question of how virtue is acquired (70a1–4) and also the Stoic doctrine that, while every human being has the potential to become good, by nature (DL 7.89), this potential comes in degrees and is

---

[59] Note that the talent under discussion here is a preferred indifferent *in the soul* (DL 7.106; cf. Stob. 2.81.19–82.4). See also *Anonymous Commentary on the Theaetetus*, col. XI (the Stoics "posit one talent underlying all the virtues"); Seneca, *Ep.* 76.30 (those who are talented [*indolis*] and well-born [*generosus*] grasp that virtue is the only good); and Cicero, *Tusc.* 4.32 (the naturally well-endowed [*ingeniosi*] are less prone to acquire psychological disease). In one suggestive report (*SVF* 3.350), Chrysippus denies that good-birth is determined by one's biological father.

[60] Thus Seneca, *Ep.* 44.5: "who is well-born (*generosus*)? He who is *by nature* well-fitted for virtue."

distributed unevenly among us: those with naturally acquired talent and good-birth would require less effort than others to attain Sagehood, although the amount of effort required for any given agent is not so large as to be humanly unattainable.[61] On the other hand, if talent and good-birth can be acquired through training and practice, as well as by nature, then there is perhaps some reason to accept that talent and good-birth will be present in every Sage: agents who lack talent and good-birth by nature can still acquire this educable condition of soul through their own patterns of behavior and habituation, and this diligence is presumably found in every virtuous person, since they will have succeeded in achieving the even more demanding goal of Sagehood itself.

At any event, we need not resolve this intra-Stoic debate here. However exactly talent and good-birth are acquired and apportioned among Sages, the Stoics speak with one voice in saying that everyone *loved* by the Sage will have these psychological features priming them to become virtuous.

3.1.2 Beauty as the Propensity for Virtue

Like talent and good-birth, the beloved's beauty, I contend, must also be a psychological condition congenial to the acquisition of virtue. This claim is controversial, since some scholars have concluded that the beauty of the Sage's beloved differs in no way from the physical characteristics conventionally prized as attractive.[62] In this section, I explain my dissatisfaction with identifying the beauty of the Sage's beloved with conventional physical beauty and argue instead that it should be understood as consisting in the psychological trait that is the propensity for virtue.

Let us begin by noting that, if the beauty of the Sage's beloved is merely physical and conventional, as some scholars suppose, then it must be ontologically distinct from the propensity for virtue. By "ontologically distinct," I mean only that the two properties are not identical: beauty, on this proposal, is a feature of the body, as opposed to talent, good-birth, and the propensity for virtue, which all pick out the same feature of the soul.[63]

---

[61] For further discussion of this background Stoic doctrine, see Bobzien 1998, 298–301, and Seneca, *Ep.* 52.5–6.

[62] For example, Bett 2010, 144: "the *kallos* in the definition [in T12] is clearly intended to refer to the physical beauty of young people . . . at the start of the relationship, the young person does not have virtue, and the beauty he or she possesses can only be beauty of the body." For the Stoics, conventional physical beauty of this kind is a preferred indifferent of the body (DL 7.106), consisting in the "symmetry of the limbs constituted with respect to each other and to the whole" (Stob. 2.63.2–3). Seneca alludes to this account of beauty at several points in the *Moral Letters*: 31.10, 33.5, 66.34. See also Čelkytė 2020, 36–8.

[63] Following other scholars, I speak of conventional beauty as "physical" or "merely physical" to denote its relationship with the body, not the soul. I do not use "physical" to mean corporeal: on this usage, the soul and its properties are equally physical as the body and its properties, since for

This observation gives rise to what Malcolm Schofield aptly calls the "Alcibiades Problem": "there is no reason why someone who exhibits the physical beauty which provokes the philosopher's desire must also be someone likely to develop into a morally admirable person" (1991, 31). According to Schofield, this problem arises in acutest form for Plato, but it arises no less acutely, we may add, for the interpreter of the Stoics who identifies the beauty of the Sage's beloved with purely physical beauty. Beauty, so construed, would seem to be the wrong feature for the wise lover to value in a prospective beloved, given the Sage's aim of making him good. Suppose that the Sage began to love a conventionally attractive but untalented youth. Such an effort could end in frustration, for even the Sage's erotic attentions could be insufficient to turn such a person to virtue and make him a friend. Yet, according to the Stoics, "nothing happens to the wise person that is contrary to his effort" (Stob. 2.115.5–7), including, we may presume, his *erotic* efforts.

Furthermore, the clear assumption in our Stoic texts is that neither beauty nor talent is ever lacking in the Sage's beloved. There is no indication, for instance, that only *some* of the Sage's beloveds are beautiful, or that only *some* are prone to acquire virtue. So perhaps physical beauty is an indicator of the aptitude for virtue – a sign of the psychological feature that the Sage really cares about in his erotic effort – or maybe the Sage erotically pursues only those youths who combine bodily beauty with a soul congenial to virtue, passing over whoever has just one of these qualities in isolation. Both interpretative possibilities have been explored, and we will evaluate them in more detail in Section 3.2. For now, though, I want to present some textual evidence in favor of my alternative proposal, on which the beauty of the Sage's beloved refers to nothing other than the beloved's propensity for virtue.

As we saw in Section 2.2, our sources move freely between speaking of the "beauty" of the Sage's beloved and her "talent" and "good-birth," raising the possibility that these terms are all co-referential. Consider again T5, which appeals to the claim that wise *erōs* is sparked by "the *beauty* belonging to young people" as a justification of "why the wise person is a lover and will love those who are worthy of love, as they are well-born and talented". This inference goes through on the assumption that the relevant kind of beauty picks out the psychological condition of being well-born and talented and worthy of

---

the Stoics all these items are corporeal (see Section 3.2.1). Moreover, even though the soul and the body it animates are both corporeal, they are not identical: the soul is separated from the body upon death (*SVF* 2.790) and interacts with it "when it is sick and being cut" (*SVF* 1.518). The Stoics thus characterize the soul and the body it animates as two ontologically distinct corporeal configurations, which are thoroughly blended together with each other (see again Section 3.2.1).

love, that is, the heightened potential for virtue. Indeed, the Stoics' more precise account of what it means to be "worthy of love" corroborates this assumption:

> **T14**: And to be "worthy of love" (*axierastos*) means the same as being "worthy of friendship" (*axiophilētos*), and not "worthy of being sexually enjoyed" (*axiapolaustos*), for being worthy of love is to be worthy of virtuous love. (Stob. 2.65.20–66.2, trans. Inwood-Gerson modified)

T14 confirms, first, that being worthy of love amounts to being talented and well-born. This is because being "worthy of love" is said to be synonymous with being "worthy of friendship", that is, worthy of being *made* a friend, on account of the relative ease with which such a person would become good through the agency of "virtuous love." Second, T14 implies that being worthy of love *is* distinct from conventional physical attractiveness, for presumably someone beautiful in this sense would be "worthy of being sexually enjoyed." So, since the Stoics maintain that the beauty of the Sage's beloved is always found together with her love-worthiness, and in light of the conceptual connection between the two properties – beauty is presumably what *makes* someone worthy of love – T14 provides support for identifying this kind of beauty with the propensity for virtue.

This construal also helps to explain why the Stoics insist that the Sage's beloved is worthy of love beyond the point at which his or her conventional good-looks have started to fade (Athenaeus, 13.563e–f). On the assumption that the Sage's beloved never fails to be beautiful, it is hard to see what would motivate this insistence, unless the kind of beauty in question is psychological. Given the educational aims of wise love, the beloved remains a suitable love-object so long as his soul is in the appropriate condition to be reformed and not fixed in its vicious ways. This psychological corrigibility is surely the reason why he is said to be "in his prime" (T5) and ripe (T6), not because his body has reached its physical peak.[64]

Consider next Zeno's "sketch" of the youth who is beautiful and worthy of love:

> **T15**: Zeno of Citium seems to sketch a certain image of a youth[65] that is beautiful and worthy of love. He sculpts him like this: Let his countenance be pure, [Zeno] says, his brow not drooping, his eyes not wide open nor half-closed,[66] his neck not thrown back, nor the limbs of his body slack, but rather

---

[64] On the "ripeness for virtue" (*anthos aretēs*, T6) and its connection to the beloved's "prime" (DL 7.130), I here follow Price 2002, 184–5, *pace* Schofield 1991, 113–14. As Price correctly insists, the phrasing of *anthos aretēs* allows that it is not virtue itself that is "flowering" in the talented youth but rather a separate set of psychological characteristics that incline him to acquire virtue. Bett's objections to this construal (2010, 145n18) raise larger issues that I address in Section 3.1.3.

[65] Reading *neaniou* with Schofield 1991, 115.

[66] Reading *anakeklasmenon* with the manuscripts and Schofield 1991, 115n3.

poised like what is taut (*meteōra entonois homoia*); his mind correctly keyed
toward sharpness in argument and holding fast to the things correctly said;
and his bearing and movements giving no hope to the licentious. (Clement,
Educator 3.11.74, trans. Schofield modified, reading Marcovich's text unless
otherwise noted)

Likely a record of Zeno's own words, T15 clarifies the sense in which the
Sage's beloved is both beautiful and worthy of love. What justifies these
descriptions, Zeno says, is not only the way in which the youth's body is
moved by his soul (graceful, modest poise in the limbs) but also his
cognitive and mental qualities (sharpness in argument and an ability to
hold fast to "the things correctly said"). Now, it is easy to see why these
psychological traits must be included, if the beauty of the Sage's beloved
consists in the propensity for virtue: dialectical skill and a good memory, for
instance, will be useful for the acquisition of the global knowledge on which
virtue rests (Section 2.1). By contrast, the inclusion of these characteristics
is highly puzzling on the supposition that his beauty is solely physical: the
conventionally attractive youth is of course very often thick-headed in
argument.[67]

3.1.3 Talent-Beauty vs. Virtue-Beauty, and Plutarch's Gnat Objection

In the previous section, I argued that the Stoic texts support a distinction
between conventional physical beauty and the beauty of the Sage's beloved,
which, like his talent, good-birth, and love-worthiness, consists in the
propensity to acquire virtue. Let us call the latter kind of beauty "talent-
beauty," to mark its psychological basis, in contrast to "conventional
beauty," which is a property of the body. That the Sage's beloved always
has talent-beauty, but not necessarily conventional beauty, explains the
insistence in our sources that wise *erōs* is directed at the soul (Athenaeus
13.563e–f; cf. *SVF* 3.721).

There is, however, another strand of thought within Stoic aesthetics linking
beauty not with the *propensity* for virtue but instead with the full-fledged

---

[67] Schofield's decision to emend the text of T15 so as to remove any reference to characteristics that
are not part of the body seems to me to beg the question about what the beauty of the Sage's
beloved consists in (1991, 115–16). My psychological reading is anticipated in Čelkytė 2020,
92–3; see also Boys-Stones 2007, 78n134. Furthermore, T15 seems to imagine the Sage's
beloved as male. Is this consistent with the Stoics' theoretical commitment to the irrelevance
of biological sex for talent-beauty (Section 2.2)? We of course have no sense of the original
context of T15 within Zeno's own writings, which may or may not have exhibited a systematic
male bias when describing the ideal beloved (cf. Athenaeus, 13.563d–e and Sextus Empiricus,
PH 3.245). In any event, it seems open to Zeno to use a male beloved *exempli gratia* in particular
contexts without compromising his more general stance that talent-beauty is found in both sexes.
I thank an anonymous referee for raising this issue.

possession of it. According to this usage, "beauty" is coextensive with "goodness." Thus we learn that "only the beautiful is good" and "everything good is beautiful," so that "the beautiful has the same force as (*isodunamon*) the good" and "is equal to it" (DL 7.101; cf. Stob. 2.78.1–6). In his accounts of Stoic ethics, Cicero translates this usage of "beautiful" (*kalon*) as *honestum* (e.g. *Fin.* 3.27, *Stoic Paradoxes* I), as does Seneca (e.g. *Ep.* 71.4, 76.10), whereas modern interpreters have "noble," "honorable," or "fine," exploiting the semantic range of the Greek original to bring out its ethical connotations. In what follows, I will call it "virtue-beauty." It is this kind of beauty that the Stoics define as the "symmetry of reason and its parts in relation to each other and to the whole" (Stob. 2.63.4–5), where the "parts of reason" will be the concepts and judgments that have been systematically organized in the mind of the Sage, so as to constitute knowledge and virtue (Cicero, *Tusc.* 4.31 and *Fin.* 3.75; Galen, *PHP* 5.3.1–3).[68]

Now, given that wise *erōs* transpires between a virtuous lover and a not yet virtuous beloved, aiming to educate the beloved so that he *becomes* virtuous as a result of the erotic effort (Section 2.2), the beauty of the Sage's beloved cannot be virtue-beauty. But given the arguments in Section 3.1.2, nor can it be mere conventional beauty either. We are therefore left with the conclusion that the Sage's beloved possesses talent-beauty, for otherwise he would fail to be beautiful at all, despite the clear implication to the contrary in our core sources. We thus do not have to accept the simple dichotomy erected by some scholars (e.g. Bett 2010, 144n17) between virtue-beauty and conventional beauty: talent-beauty is a third option recognized by the Stoics, and the Sage's beloved is always beautiful in this specific sense.

The Stoics' careful aesthetic distinctions are muddled in Plutarch's objection to wise *erōs* (*Com. Not.* 1072e–1073c; *St. Ab. Poet.* 1058a). According to Plutarch, the Stoic account of the Sage's love violates our "common concepts" – roughly, our shared, authoritative intuitions[69] – regarding the relationship between *erōs* and beauty. What motivates Plutarch's objection, however, is the dubious inference that since the Sage's beloved lacks virtue-beauty, he is therefore beautiful *in no respect*: virtue-beauty is thus the only form of beauty

---

[68] The Stoic sources do not observe a neat distinction between *kalos* and *kallos*, such that the former always and only refers to virtue-beauty. For instance, *kallos* is the term used to explicate virtue-beauty at Stob. 2.63.4–5, and *kalos* appears in Zeno's account of the talent-beauty of the Sage's beloved in T15. See also T7, on the Sage correctly ordering the beautiful (*kalon*) but not yet virtuous. Consequently, it is up to the interpreter to assess what sense of "beauty" is in play when either Greek term is used (and likewise with the Latin terms *formosus* and *pulcher*). For detailed discussion of virtue-beauty in the Stoic sources, see Čelkytė 2020, 50–70.

[69] On the relation between intuitions and common concepts in Hellenistic philosophy, and especially in the context of Academic-Stoic debates, see Ierodiakonou 2022.

Plutarch allows the Stoics to recognize.[70] He then proceeds to draw a series of counterintuitive conclusions following on from the unqualified ugliness of the not yet virtuous beloved. First, the Stoics are charged with contravening our common concept by directing wise *erōs* at what is ugly, since the Sage's beloved "is base and lacking intelligence" (*Com. Not.* 1073a). Second, Plutarch asserts that it is illegitimate to call such a person "worthy of love" (*axierastos*), if he is only expected to become beautiful later on but lacks beauty at present (*Com. Not.* 1073b). And third, the educational aim of wise *erōs* implies that this effort will end as soon as the beloved becomes genuinely beautiful, that is, as soon as he acquires virtue (*Com. Not.* 1073a). This "horrifying" (*deinos*) implication prompts Plutarch to compare wise lovers to "gnats, for they delight in scum and vinegar but fly from and avoid palatable and fine wine" (*Com. Not.* 1073a), and to "beetles [which] are said to leave perfume and to pursue foul-smelling things," since "Stoic *erōs* consorts with the ugliest and most unshapely and turns away when these are transformed into shapeliness and beauty by wisdom" (*St. Ab. Poet.* 1058a).

Plutarch's "gnat objection," as I will call these interconnected points of critique, unfairly saddles the Stoics with an impoverished aesthetic account, on which the only kind of beauty is virtue-beauty, but in other respects is not entirely misleading. For instance, Plutarch justifiably understands the possession of virtue-beauty as an all-or-nothing affair, since it rests on knowledge (Section 2.1): when it comes to virtue-beauty, one is either a fully beautiful Sage or a fully ugly non-Sage. Plutarch is therefore also correct to insist that if there is anything grounding the love-worthiness of the Sage's beloved, it cannot be that he already possesses virtue-beauty. Moreover, the account of wise *erōs* invoked at *Com. Not.* 1073b – "a kind of hunt (*thera tis*) after a youth who is incomplete but talented for virtue" – chimes well with the rest of our Stoic evidence.[71] And it is not implausible to locate the end point of virtuous love at the moment the beloved becomes good (Section 2.2). However, in supposing that the Sage's beloved is ugly *without qualification* so long as he lacks virtue-beauty, Plutarch suppresses the well-attested tendency of the Stoics to posit another condition of soul, falling short of virtue and thus open to the non-Sage, as genuinely beautiful: talent-beauty. More precisely, then, the Sage's *erōs* is directed at something ugly in one sense (*qua* lacking virtue) but beautiful in

---

[70] Consider *St. Ab. Poet.* 1058a: the Stoic "Sage, though remaining hunchbacked, if he so happens to be, and toothless and one-eyed, is not ugly or misshapen or unhandsome of face." The translation of the Plutarch texts in this paragraph and the next is based on Cherniss'.

[71] Note the hunting language in the account of erotic virtue in T3, and the formulation "talented for virtue" in T6.

another (*qua* talented), and this result is arguably consistent with the intuition embedded in our common concept that *erōs* is a response to beauty.

Plutarch is not the only critic of Stoic *erōs* who elides the school's delicate distinctions among different forms of beauty. Consider this terse argument formulated by Sextus Empiricus, parodying the style of the early Stoics:

[i] The person worthy of love is beautiful.
[ii] But only the Sage is worthy of love.
[iii] Therefore, only the Sage is beautiful. (*M.* 11.170–1)

The Stoics would be willing to accept the truth of premise [i] and the conclusion [iii], provided that "beautiful" picks out different features in each occurrence: talent-beauty in [i] and virtue-beauty in [iii].[72] Sextus' argument thus equivocates. Moreover, premise [ii] comes out false on the Stoics' most exact account of what it means to be "worthy of love," that is, worthy of being made a friend through the agency of virtuous love (T14).[73] As Plutarch correctly saw, wise love is not a response to virtue-beauty, and the Sage does not have *erōs* for another Sage (Section 2.2). What Plutarch failed to mention, however, is that Sages are joined in mutual friendship (*philia*) and thus not emotionally inert in the face of virtue-beauty, so that the end point of a successful erotic effort does not imply a total break in positive, intimate feelings between the Sage and his former beloved.

3.2 The Direct Perception of Talent-Beauty

Section 3.1 presented a case for taking the beauty of the Sage's beloved to refer to her propensity for virtue. In this section, I take up an objection to this proposal, centered on the role of the perception of beauty as the initial cause of wise love.

One might think that conventional physical beauty is the only type of beauty that could incite an "impression of beauty" (T8, T12), or be "made to appear" (T5–T7), in the mind of the Sage. So in order to detect talent and the aptitude for virtue in a prospective beloved, the Sage would have to *infer*, on the basis of perceiving someone to be conventionally attractive, that such a person also has a soul that is readily made good through a long-term erotic effort. This kind of inferential model is endorsed by several scholars. Martha Nussbaum, for

---

[72] As argued in Section 3.1.2, T5 and T14 ground the love-worthiness of the Sage's beloved in her talent-beauty. Cicero includes [iii] among the Stoic Paradoxes (*Acad.* 2.136), and so we can safely interpret [iii] as the claim that virtue-beauty is found in the Sage alone: see also DL 7.100 and Alexander of Aphrodisias, *SVF* 3.594.

[73] Here I agree with Schofield's assessment of Sextus' premise [ii] (1991, 113n1), *pace* Bett 2010, 142.

instance, writes that the Stoic account of wise *erōs* "gives the sight of beauty a central causal role," such that "the wise man will reason that what he finds so moving is not really the bodily beauty, but the signs of the soul within" (1998, 291–2). Similarly, according to Richard Bett, the Sage is attracted to physical beauty "as an outward sign of the person's potential for virtue" (2010, 145). These scholars agree, then, that conventional beauty serves as a defeasible, if not infallible, indicator of talent, allowing the Sage to infer from this directly perceptible feature which person is most likely to benefit from her erotic attention.[74]

This type of inferential model faces a textual difficulty, however, even if we grant the implausible conjecture that conventional beauty is some-how positively correlated with the propensity for virtue. In his sketch of the beautiful youth who is worthy of love (T15), Zeno does not focus on the static condition of the body as such – on the symmetrical profile of the body parts that determines physical beauty (Stob. 2.63.2–3) – but rather on such features as *motion* and *bearing* – how the body is *moved* by the soul – and on other plainly psychological qualities pertaining to memory and dialectical skill (Section 3.1.2). As we will see momentarily, Zeno's emphasis here is not at all unusual among Stoic texts, and it points to an important Stoic commitment, which, I will argue, dispenses with the need for the elaborate inferential model endorsed by the scholars above. I will show that, from Zeno onwards, the Stoics understand character traits and other psychological qualities as *directly perceptible*, so that the propensity for virtue need not be inferred from physical beauty but instead is immediately revealed in the Sage's expert impression of the beloved's talent-beauty.

3.2.1 "Character Can Be Grasped from Form"

Let us begin with this passage of Chrysippus:

> **T16**: And Chrysippus says that goods and bads are perceptible, writing the following in book one of *On Goals*: "for even with the following one has enough to assert that goods and bads are perceptible. For not only are the passions perceptible, including their species, for instance grief and fear etc., but also it is possible to perceive theft and adultery and similar things and, in general, thoughtlessness and cowardice and not a few other vices – and not

---

[74] See further Nussbaum 1998, 292: "we can't tell whether all physical beauty is taken to be the sign of this aptitude [for virtue], but the Stoics appear to think that it is necessary that some beauty be present"; and Bett 2010, 145: "there is a connection between physical beauty – or at least, some instances of physical beauty – and an inner potential for developing the beauty of soul that goes along with virtue." Compare Laurand 2007, 79–80.

only joy and correct actions and many other virtuous actions, but also prudence and courage and the rest of the virtues." (Plutarch, *St. Rep.* 1042e–f, trans. Cherniss modified)

To establish the general conclusion that "goods and bads are perceptible," Chrysippus here employs an argument by cases. Elsewhere, the Stoics divide up what is good between virtues and virtuous actions (Stob. 2.58.5–9) and, analogously, what is bad between vices and vicious actions (Stob. 2.58.14–18). The general conclusion follows, then, from the claim (i) that both types of bad are perceptible – vicious actions (such as the passions and "theft and adultery and similar things") as well as the vices – and (ii) that both types of good are perceptible ("not only joy and correct actions and many other virtuous actions, but also prudence and courage and the rest of the virtues"). The perceptibility of virtuous and vicious actions may strike one as the less controversial claim here: to perceptually judge that a token action is an instance of fear, for example, would seem to be relatively straightforward, in contrast to seeing cowardice itself. Chrysippus does not indicate, however, that virtuous and vicious actions are somehow *more perceptible* than the virtues and vices themselves, nor that actions are directly perceptible but the dispositions only indirectly so: on the contrary, with respect to their perceptibility, actions and dispositions are here set on a par.

To see the motivation for Chrysippus' contention that virtues and vices are directly perceptible, we must first take note of the metaphysical status of these dispositions. The Stoics maintain that the soul and its qualities are corporeal entities, since they act upon the underlying human body that they animate and are acted upon in turn.[75] More precisely, the soul is said to be made up of "breath" (*pneuma*) (DL 7.157) – a fiery-airy substance vibrating in tensile motion – with the virtues "the same in substance," so that "every virtue is a body and is called a body, for the mind and soul are bodies" (Stob. 2.64.19–24). Indeed, further sources confirm the corporeality of psychological qualities in general, not just the virtues specifically (Iamblichus, *SVF* 2.826; Seneca, *Ep.* 106.6–10). Given their corporeality, then, the soul and its qualities are in principle able to make contact with, and be registered by, the sense-organs in the same way as ordinary external objects.

Of course, the corporeality, and hence perceptibility, of psychological conditions is a thesis about the *embodied* human soul. In defending the possibility

---

[75] So argues Cleanthes (in Nemesius, *SVF* 1.518) and Chrysippus (in Nemesius, *SVF* 2.790). For the activity of the virtues in particular, see Stob. 2.65.1–6. Cf. Seneca, *Ep.* 106.4 and 117.2, where the activity of goods in general consists in providing benefit, from which Seneca concludes they are bodies. In what follows I build on the important work of Schofield 1991, 31–2.

of perceiving (e.g.) "prudence and courage and the rest of the virtues" (T16),
Chrysippus clearly has in view the dispositions of a soul blended together with,
and acting upon, a particular configuration of flesh and blood: the psychological qualities of a living person, in other words.[76] It is a mistake, however,
to suppose that in perceiving the motion and bearing of the living body – the
way it is directed by the corporeal soul intermingled with and ruling over it –
the body alone is all that one can see. Rather, Chrysippus insists that in such
cases it is also possible to perceive the *soul itself* at work. For Zeno and
Cleanthes too, in perceiving the form that a living person displays in motion
and activity, one can also perceive the character of the soul causally respon-
sible for such motion:

> **T17**: It is said that some young men set out to play a trick on Cleanthes, who
> followed Zeno in claiming that character can be grasped from form. They
> brought to him a man who was sexually deviant, but toughened up through his
> work in the fields, and they demanded that Cleanthes should declare his
> character. He could not make it out, and he told the man to go away. But as
> the man was going, he sneezed, and Cleanthes said, "I have him! He's
> dissolute". (DL 7.173, trans. Boys-Stones modified)

T17 implicitly contrasts two sets of properties of the agrarian deviant: (1) the
static features of his body (e.g. the calloused skin on his feet and hands,
characteristic of tough field work) and (2) the way he moves while sneezing.
Limited to (1), Cleanthes fails to vindicate the Zenonian claim that "character
can be grasped from form" (*katalēpton einai to ēthos ex eidous*); he cannot on
the basis of (1) "declare his character." Rather, it is only when Cleanthes has
perceived (2), the motion and bearing of the agrarian, that his dissolute condition becomes apparent and is grasped. We saw the same emphasis on movement
in Zeno's sketch (T15), suggesting that the "form" through which character is
revealed consists in the outward appearance of the person *over time*, in the look
of his gestures and behavior. Thus George Boys-Stones concludes – correctly, in
my view – that the Stoics differ from traditional physiognomists in eschewing
the "natural geography of the physical body" as a basis for determining psychological character (2007, 79–80).[77] Elsewhere, the Stoics speak of character
(*ēthos*) as the "spring of life, from which particular actions flow" (Stob.
2.38.15–17), and they accept that a vicious character "fills out form"
(Plutarch, *Com. Not.* 1073b). The crucial Stoic claim, then, is that psychological
traits – whatever their moral quality – always manifest in the way a living

---

[76] On the total intermixture of soul and body in living human beings, see e.g. Hierocles, *Elements of Ethics* III.55–IV.15, IV.38–53.

[77] This point is missed by Laurand 2007, 80, and Collette-Dučić, who asserts that "the Stoics acknowledged physiognomics as a science" (2014, 94).

person is conducted in action and motion. So, by attending to these *kinetic* features of form, it is possible to grasp – perceptually and immediately – what kind of soul is causing them.

Further texts corroborate T17's suggestion that psychological character is invariably exhibited in, and so directly graspable from, motion and bearing (the person's "form"). One dimension of the Sage's virtuous disposition is orderliness (*kosmiotēs*), or "the knowledge of which movements are fitting" (Stob. 2.115.12–14), and another is calmness (*hēsuchiotēs*), "the proper organization (*eutaxia*) of states of motion and rest of the soul and body in accordance with nature" (Stob. 2.115.14–16). Given the cooperation of the virtues (Section 2.1), orderliness and calmness contribute to every action the Sage performs, so that she always carries herself with a recognizable and determinate bearing, one that fits whatever scenario she finds herself in. For this reason, the Stoics declare, the Sage is able to be grasped as such through perception, her form serving as proof (*SVF* 1.204).[78]

Moreover, just after explaining the corporeality of vices and vicious actions, Seneca turns to virtues and virtuous actions, arguing that they too are bodies:

> **T18**: Do you not see how much energy is given to the eyes by courage? How steady a gaze is given by prudence? How much mildness and calmness is given by reverence? How tranquil a demeanor is given by joy? How much firmness is given by strict self-discipline? How much relaxation by gentleness? So, the things which alter the form and condition (*colorem habitumque*) of bodies and exercise their dominion in bodies are themselves bodies. (Seneca, *Ep.* 106.7, trans. Inwood modified)

Seneca here enumerates the changes in the Sage's motions – alterations in her "form and condition" – that are brought about through the agency of virtuous character-traits (prudence, courage, etc.) and virtuous actions (joy). Since these goods "exercise dominion" over the wise person's body – that is, are in contact with it and are causally efficacious over it, changing her movement in definite ways – Seneca concludes that virtues and virtuous actions are corporeal, in line with orthodox Stoic doctrine. Note, however, that T18's argument for the corporeality of virtues and virtuous actions also lends support to their perceptibility.[79] The manner in which (e.g.) courage causally interacts with and governs the "energy" of the eyes is a kinetic feature that is straightforwardly detectable by a keen perceiver.

---

[78] The Sage is also said to have removed any phoniness (*plasma*) from her voice and form (DL 7.118). Perhaps, then, the Stoics would be prepared to say that virtuous character can be grasped through hearing as well as vision. Their claim, after all, is that goods of this kind are *perceptible* (T16), and character *graspable* (T17), not merely *visible*, even though visual cases are clearly their main focus. (However, I know of no text testifying to the distinctive scent, taste, or haptic feel of the Sage's form.)

[79] Thus Inwood 2007, 268–9.

Consider next Cicero's account of the perceptibility of character:

> **T19**: All the human senses far surpass those of animals. For, in the first place,
> they discern with subtlety many things in the realm of expertise, for which the
> eyes are the judge, like painting, modeling, and sculpture, and also in bodily
> motion and gesture (*corporum etiam motione atque gestu*); for there the eyes
> judge elegance of form and shape (*colorum etiam et figurarum tum venusta-
> tem*), as well as orderliness and, so to speak, propriety (*decentia*), not to
> mention even greater qualities; for they recognize virtues and vices, and also
> someone who is angry or friendly, joyful or sad, brave or a coward, bold or
> timid. (Cicero, *On the Nature of the Gods* 2.145, trans. Walsh modified)

Like T17 and T18, T19 identifies "bodily motion and gesture" as the vehicle
through which psychological traits are exhibited and perceived: it is there
(*tum*), our Stoic spokesman emphasizes, that one is able to perceptually
"judge elegance of form and shape" as well as the causal presence of virtue
or vice.

Note further the range of character-traits that T19 claims to be perceptible in
this way: not only the virtues and vices but also psychological conditions such
as irascibility and timidity ("someone who is angry ... or timid"). Margaret
Graver calls these "scalar conditions of mind," since, unlike virtue and vice,
they come in degrees (2007: 133–48): although every non-Sage is equally
vicious, some may be prone to anger or fear more than others (Stob. 2.93.1–
13); and, analogously, although every Sage is equally virtuous, some may be
fond of literature or music more than others (Stob. 2.67.5–12).[80] The Stoics are
clear, however, that all these psychological traits are corporeal (Iamblichus,
SVF 2.826; Seneca, *Ep.* 106.6–10) and, hence, perceptible – as T19 confirms
explicitly (so also Seneca, *Ep.* 52.12 and 114.3). The perceptibility of scalar
conditions arguably falls out of T17 as well, if we understand the character-trait
revealed in the agrarian's sneeze as a kind of sexual dissipation to which some
vicious agents are subject more than others.[81] Plutarch is oversimplifying the

---

[80] I take these examples from the sources. All vicious agents are said to possess the disposition
(*diathesis*) of vice, but to differ in their conditions (*hexeis*) or traits (*ēthē*) of character. For the
Stoic distinction between dispositions and conditions, see Simplicius, *Cat.* 8.237–8, and Stob.
2.70.21–71.14. In the case of the non-Sage, included among the scalar conditions of mind are
psychological diseases, on which see Shogry 2021 and Section 2.3.1. Regarding virtuous agents,
all are said to possess the disposition (*diathesis*) of virtue, but to differ in their "habits"
(*epitēdeumata*) – a kind of condition (*hexis*) – for example, fondness of literature or music
(Stob. 2.70.21–71.3). One text refers to these habits and other forms of expertise as "quasi-
virtues" (Stob. 2.73.1–15).

[81] See Boys-Stones 2007, 78n133. One scalar condition of mind attested for the non-Sage clearly
relates to sex: the psychological disease of women-madness (*gunaikomania*: Galen, *PHP*
4.5.19–23; Athenaeus 11.464d). Compare the "erotic disposition" associated with intemperance
in Clement, *SVF* 2.346, and the erotic proclivity mentioned in Cicero, *Tusc.* 4.27. Moreover, at

Stoic position, then, in suggesting that only *vices* "fill out form" (*Com. Not.* 1073b): scalar conditions, not to mention the virtues, do so as well.

For present purposes, it is important to stress the general scope of the Stoic thesis that character is perceptible, since the propensity for virtue will be one such scalar condition. Among non-Sages who are not yet virtuous, some will be more prone to acquire virtue than others (cf. T13), and this character-trait – talent – will be directly perceptible just like any other.

This conclusion sheds new light on T15 and puts it into its proper theoretical context. Consistent with his more general claim that "character can be grasped from form," Zeno here sketches the ways in which the specific psychological quality that is talent-beauty manifests in, and is immediately revealed together with, the motion and bearing of the youth. T6, one of our core sources for wise *erōs*, also comes into clearer view, in particular its claim that "the wise man will love young people who create an impression, *through their form*, of a talent for virtue."[82] As we can now appreciate, "form" here must have the same sense as in T17–T19. The aptitude for virtue is thus a corporeal psychological trait that causally determines the ways in which the youth comports himself in motion and action – just like courage governs the energy of the Sage's eyes (T18), or sexual dissolution, the motion of the agrarian's sneeze (T17) – and, in altering his form, is directly perceptible.

Before examining in more detail the "impression" mentioned in T6, I will close this section by clarifying how my reconstruction differs from the rival inferential model set out above (Section 3.2). According to this model, the only type of beauty that is directly perceptible is conventional physical beauty, from which the Sage infers that a prospective beloved is likely to have the potential for virtue, a non-perceptible feature of soul. But since it is not only static states of the body that are perceptible, on the Stoic view, the Sage does not have to rely on any such probabilistic mental process to detect talent. The aptitude for virtue is directly perceptible along with the kinetic features of the beloved that constitute his form: these features of bearing and comportment are necessarily found together with talent as its causal manifestation. Indeed, Seneca goes so far as to deny that the manifestations of talent could ever be perfectly imitated by an actor (*Ep.* 11.1–7).

Now, one might object that, on my account, the Sage is also making an inference, just on the basis of a broader set of information than the rival model envisions, namely the motion and bearing of the beloved rather than

---

Ep. 114.4, Seneca claims that the wanton (*delicatus*) character of a certain Maecenas could be perceptually detected in his gait and style of speech.

[82] Emphasis mine: καὶ ἐρασθήσεσθαι δὲ τὸν σοφὸν τῶν νέων τῶν ἐμφαινόντων διὰ τοῦ εἴδους τὴν πρὸς ἀρετὴν εὐφυΐαν. I defend my translation of ἐμφαινόντων in the next section.

his static shape. However, as I have stressed, the Stoics maintain that talent and other psychological traits are in principle perceptible, just like any other corporeal entity. But while it is easy to see, in some cases, the causal agent together with the causal patient it is altering – for instance, the potter's hands shaping the wet clay on the wheel, or the back-and-forth rocking of a bread loaf as it is being sawed by a knife – to perceive what kind of soul is at work in guiding the motion of a human body requires some special expertise: *erotic expertise*, as the Stoics will call it. It is to this issue that I now turn.

3.2.2 Erotic Expertise and Expert Impressions of Talent

To better understand the non-inferential character of the Sage's perception of talent in the beloved, it is useful to survey the Stoics' broader theoretical interest in the interaction between expertise and perception – more precisely, between expertise and the sense-impressions the expert forms.

In general, sense-impressions function as information-carrying modifications of the mind – psychological states responsible for bringing external objects and their features into the agent's awareness (Chrysippus, *SVF* 2.54). So, for instance, suppose that on a visit to the Louvre I happen upon the *Mona Lisa*. The sense-impression is the psychological state I automatically create that enables me to consciously attend to the painting and appreciate its sensory characteristics (e.g. its color, shape, and size). The Stoics classify sense-impressions in various, crosscutting ways – according to their truth-value, persuasiveness, epistemological reliability, and so on (cf. Sextus Empiricus, *M.* 7.241–8) – but one such classification deserves special attention here:

> **T20**: Some impressions are expert (*technikē*), others inexpert (*atechnos*). A picture, then, will be observed in one way by the expert and in another way by the non-expert. (DL 7.51, trans. Long and Sedley modified)

On the Stoic account, expertise is a cognitive achievement that improves the way one sees the world. T20 implies that, when the art-historian encounters a painting – or any other skilled person (*technikos*), an object falling within their domain of specialization – the sense-impression she forms is richer in content than the one formed by the amateur. So whereas I, lacking expertise in Italian Renaissance art, notice only that the *Mona Lisa* is smiling and that the background color is greenish, the art-historian sees the use of *sfumato* technique in its composition and the detail in the depiction of her hands. Here the Stoic claim is not merely that the art-historian and amateur form different *judgments* about the painting; we *perceive* it differently too.[83]

This commitment is important for present purposes, since the Stoics posit the existence of *erotic expertise* (*erōtikē technē*), on which Zeno and Cleanthes each wrote a full treatise (DL 7.34, 175). We can surmise that this expertise is one facet of the Sage's erotic virtue, which, according to T3, consists in the "knowledge of how to hunt for talented young people, which turns them to virtue – and, in general, [in] the knowledge of loving well." Such a hunt will be aided by the perceptual ability to detect which young people are talented, and my suggestion here is that the Sage is able to do so as a consequence of her possession of erotic expertise. Whenever she meets with a person of talent and observes their form, the Sage generates an expert sense-impression that this person is beautiful and worthy of love. We can thus understand erotic expertise as a kind of science of human form: its domain ranges over the causal manifest-ations of the psychological character-traits relevant for a successful erotic effort, above all talent-beauty. If this is right, then not just any perceiver will be able to see the propensity for virtue in motion and bearing – or, more generally, to grasp character from form. However, like other kinds of expertise, such an ability is teachable, and Zeno's interest in sketching "an image of a youth that is beautiful and worthy of love" (T15) should be understood as an attempt in that direction.

That expertise is sometimes required to perceive character-traits is confirmed by the Stoic Hierocles:

> **T21**: Someone who is good at judging characters, if he stands next to people in their sleep, will be able to recognize, on the basis of his manner of sleeping, what kind of disposition the sleeper has – whether it is strong and full of tension or else more dissolute than it should be. (Hierocles, *Elements of Ethics* col. V, lines 11–15, trans. Konstan modified)

Note that "dissolution" is the vicious character-trait perceptually detected by Cleanthes in T17. T21 underscores that such scalar psychological conditions manifest even in sleep: the causal activity of the corporeal soul and its qualities is constant and never fully latent in regulating the motion of the body.[84] However, only someone "good at judging characters" – that is, in possession of the relevant expertise – is able to form an impression that discloses these psychological causes alongside the changes in the body which they bring about.

---

[83] See, for example, Shogry 2021, 793–5, for further discussion of expert impressions in Stoicism.

[84] I assume that Hierocles uses "disposition" (*diathesis*) in T21 broadly, so that it covers both scalar and non-scalar traits of character.

One might object to my reconstruction here on the grounds that we nowhere find the language of "impression" (*phantasia*) in our core sources for wise *erōs*, and so it is doubtful that the Stoics intend to invoke their account of expert impressions in this context. This objection is mistaken, however. The use of *emphainein* and cognate terms in the main accounts of wise love (T5–T7) serves to indicate that the wise lover will form an impression (*phantasia*) of the beloved. This is because the Stoics sometimes use *emphasis* synonymously with *phantasia*.[85] Literally, *emphainein* means "to make something appear in something"; we can therefore understand *emphasis* to refer to the product of this process.[86] I thus read *kallos emphainomenon* in T5–T7 as "the beauty which has been made to appear" or "the beauty which has been impressed," namely in the mind of the wise lover on the basis of her encounter with a talented beloved. This is equivalent to T12's formulation, "an impression of beauty" (*kallous emphasin*), and underlies Cicero's decision to translate this phrase into Latin as *pulchritudinis species* (T8), where *species* has the sense of "that which appears in the mind": it is the beloved's talent-beauty that so appears to the Sage.[87]

Nothing prevents us, then, from deploying the Stoics' highly developed theory of expert impressions to explicate the core sources of wise *erōs*. According to this theory, the degree to which an agent has refined her rationality is reflected in the detail of the impressions she creates. This is because to form an impression is itself an activity of reason, on the Stoic view (DL 7.51). Impressions are not purely passive changes in the sense-organs but rather products of the perceiver's intellect, the result of its interpretation and articulation of the deliverances of the sense-organs (Sextus Empiricus, *M.* 7.232–3) on the basis of the concepts and judgments the perceiver has built up over time.

Consider the following example. A musical expert and amateur hear the same piece, in the same auditory conditions. Here the Stoics claim that, in response to the same auditory input, the impressions generated by these two perceivers will differ (Cicero, *Acad.* 2.20). The expert receives a "scientific perception"

---

[85] Epictetus uses *phantasia* and *emphasis* interchangeably to refer to the mental representation one has of beauty (*Diss.* 4.11.25–30). See further DL 7.51 and Sextus Empiricus, *M.* 10.300, with discussion in Reinhardt 2019, 228–9. Collette-Dučić proposes that *emphasis* is a special kind of *phantasia* (2014, 91–3). However, this specific usage of *emphasis* is not always maintained, as we see in Sextus Empiricus, *M.* 10.300, where *emphasis* is used no more determinately than *phantasia*.

[86] Thus Reinhardt 2019, 229n30. Compare Bett 2010, 141n12, replying to Schofield 1991, 112–13, and Price 2002, 184.

[87] Compare Lewis and Short s.v. *species* II.A.3, and Cicero, *Off.* 3.81. I thus follow Graver 2002 in translating *pulchritudinis species* in T8 as "impression of beauty." Alternatively, we might render *pulchritudinis species* as the "form of beauty," on the assumption that *species* is Cicero's translation of *eidos* in T6. On this construal, *species* would be a property of the beloved – her form, that is, her pattern of motion of bearing – rather than a psychological state in the mind of the Sage created on the basis of perceiving that form.

(*epistēmonikē aisthēsis*) of a genuine property of the music, while the nonexpert does not (Philodemus, *On Music* IV col. 34, lines 1–8). The expert's achievements in the domain of music are thus registered in the content of her impression of the piece. What her ears convey to her mind is filtered through the specialized concepts and grasps she has obtained as a result of her expert training. So, for instance, she will receive the impression that *This melody is in the Dorian mode* or *This rhythm is syncopated*, whereas the amateur hears only that *This song sounds sad*. Here the musician need not make any non-perceptual inference to access the contents of her expert impressions: they are immediately revealed in her rationally infused sensory experience.

Analogously, let us now consider a case where the same talented individual is observed by two perceivers, one of whom is ordinarily vicious whereas the other is a Sage in full possession of erotic virtue and erotic expertise. Let us further suppose that the talented individual in question is conventionally ugly. In watching the movement of such a person's face, the poise of his limbs and gait, and other aspects of his bearing, the erotic expert creates the impression that *This person has talent-beauty*, or *This person's movements are being produced by the aptitude for virtue*, whereas the ordinary agent sees only that *This person is hideous*. It is this expert perceptual discrimination, enabled by the cognitive achievements distinctive of erotic expertise – including a grasp of beauty that extends beyond the physical to embrace the propensity for virtue – that leads the Sage to initiate an erotic effort. Indeed, this analysis provides a further reason to restrict the effort definition to wise *erōs* (Section 2.4): the type of beauty justifying the effort to gain friendship – talent-beauty – cannot be made to appear in the mind of the erotic amateur.

4 Socratic Antecedents for the Stoic Theory of *Erōs*

To what extent is the Stoic theory of *erōs* Socratic in inspiration? My contention in this section is that Socratic thinking on *erōs* – specifically, the account Socrates presents in Plato's *Symposium* and there credits to the mysterious priestess Diotima – anticipates the Stoic theory in construing *erōs* as a psychological state admitting of expertise, which motivates the lover to pursue what she takes to be good, beautiful, and productive of happiness. In emphasizing this Socratic link, I depart from the scholarly consensus, which recognizes the *Symposium* as a formative text for the Stoa but identifies Pausanias, not Socrates, as the speaker in the dialogue who most directly influences the Stoic treatment of *erōs*.[88] I will show that the similarities between the Stoics and

---

[88] Foucault 1990, 199, followed by Inwood 1997, 56–60, Nussbaum 1998, 289–93, Gaca 2000, 212–14, and Gill 2013, 146. See also Collette-Dučić 2014, 95–8. Laurand 2007 is an outlier here,

Pausanias are superficial at most, and that, on closer inspection, Pausanias' outlook rests on assumptions the Stoics would find deeply objectionable. To be sure, the Stoics differ from the *Symposium*'s Socrates in important ways, above all in their rejection of an intelligible Form of Beauty, perfect, eternal, and separate from the sensible objects that partake of beauty to a greater or lesser extent but never without qualification. Nonetheless, I will suggest that these metaphysical commitments – seen as problematic by the Stoics – were also viewed as detachable from the moral psychology they understood as character-istically Socratic and utilized in so many areas of their ethical system, no less than in their theory of love.

Before I begin, a word to justify my approach. I am not here pursuing the unanswerable question of how the *historical* Socrates inspired the Stoic account of *erōs*, but instead the more tractable one of how the Platonic depiction of him in the *Symposium* – and, in turn, that depiction's depiction of Diotima – could have done so. In other words, what theoretical resources *could* the Stoics have recovered from Socrates' speech and employed in the service of crafting their own theory of *erōs*? Nonetheless, one might wonder why I do not concentrate on other Platonic dialogues in which the character Socrates discusses *erōs* at length. Socrates' palinode in the *Phaedrus* strikes me as an unpromising source for Stoic theory, for several reasons: (i) the Stoics reject erotic madness as the model for the best form of love (T3);[89] (ii) they are unsympathetic to the tripartite theory of the soul and see no need to posit the existence of non-rational desires to explain the nature of *erōs* in human agents (cf. *Phaedrus* 253c–255a); and (iii) they have little theoretical interest in "reciprocal love" (*anterōs*: *Phaedrus* 255d–e), since wise love is asymmetrical on their account and cannot arise between two Sages.[90] Moreover, Socrates does not thematize madness, tripartition, and reciprocal love in the *Symposium*, and, though both dialogues appeal to Forms, their appearance in *Symposium* does not prevent Stoic engage-ment with other parts of Socrates' account there (or so I will argue). Plato's *Lysis* has Socrates invoke erotic expertise (204b7–c2), a claim I address in Section 4.2, but otherwise focuses on friendship, and so I set it aside. Of course, Plato is not the only author of extant Socratic dialogues. Socrates' portrayal in

---

but his case against Pausanian influence differs from mine and relies on a questionable construal of the core sources of Stoic *erōs*. Note that Plato is mentioned as an authority for the Stoic position in T8.

[89] Here the Stoic view is closer to Socrates' in *Republic* 3.403a10–11: "the right kind of love has nothing mad (*manikon*) or licentious about it." Note also that some manuscript readings of DL 7.130 have the Stoics deny that love is "god-sent" (*theopempton*): compare *Phaedrus* 245b1–2 and Nussbaum 1998, 292.

[90] We find *anterōs* and its cognates nowhere in *SVF*. It seems possible for two *vicious* agents to feel *erōs* for each other, but such relationships are not theorized in our sources under the label of "reciprocal love". Here I agree with Nussbaum 1998, 293–4.

Xenophon's *Symposium* will be floated as an alternative origin for Stoic ideas that other scholars too quickly attribute to Pausanias (Section 4.2). Overall, however, my aim is to make a case for taking Socrates' speech in the *Symposium* as the most theoretically fecund starting point available to the Stoics, even though they depart from him on the metaphysics of beauty and its wider implications.

4.1 *Erōs* as Cognitive-cum-Motivational State

Throughout his speech in the *Symposium*, Socrates characterizes *erōs* as a state that combines motivation and evaluative cognition: it is a form of desire that is guided by and inseparable from the agent's views of what is good, beautiful, and productive of happiness.

Socrates works up to this account in stages. First, he secures his host Agathon's agreement that love has an object, and that love desires its object (200a2–4). *Erōs* is therefore a motivational state. It impels the lover to pursue what he lacks at present (200e3–201a1). Later on, it is agreed that these objects, which the lover lacks and desires, are both beautiful and good, for love is constitutively related to the beautiful (201a2–10), and the beautiful is coextensive with the good (201c1–2; cf. 204e1–2).

In labeling the objects of *erōs* as good and beautiful, Socrates has in mind the description under which they are desired by the lover. It is because the lover believes or perceives or otherwise cognizes that x is good and beautiful that he loves x. So love is understood as a cognitively loaded desire, one that always involves and rests on a form of evaluative cognition: *erōs* motivates the lover to seek the objects he considers good and beautiful *because* they are considered good and beautiful. We observe a similar usage of "good" in the *Meno*. There, in explicating his proposal that "everyone desires good things" (77c1–2), Socrates appeals to the idea that the good things in question are those that the agent believes to be good (77d7–e4), not necessarily the things that are in fact good. It is not fully clear, however, whether Socrates in the *Symposium* affirms the view in the *Meno* that *all* forms of desire are dependent upon the agent's beliefs about the good, or whether he is instead making the narrower proposal that only *erōs* is cognitively infused in this way (thus leaving open the possibility that desires other than *erōs* arise independently of the agent's evaluative beliefs).[91] We need not settle this controversy here, as the crucial point for now is the tight connection, identified in the *Symposium*, between the lover's views about what is good and beautiful and the objects he

---

[91] See Sheffield 2006, 227–39, for incisive discussion of this issue. Commentators who find continuity with *Meno* include Price 1997, 254–5, and Rowe 2006, whereas the narrower interpretation is accepted by, for example, Irwin 1995, 303n12, and Wedgwood 2009, 307–8.

loves: "*erōs*" is Socrates' name for the desire that leads the agent to pursue the objects cognized as good and beautiful.

That the good and beautiful objects *erōs* desires are also those that the lover thinks will produce *happiness* emerges in the next phase of Socrates' speech, when he recounts the theory he learned from Diotima. Here Socrates comes to see, on the basis of Diotima's questioning, that love is the desire for good things, more precisely, the desire to possess them, and in possessing good things one is made happy (204e1–205a4; cf. 202c10–11). Love thus turns out to be the desire for happiness – or, equivalently, the "wish" (*boulēsis*) to be happy (Socrates seems to use "desire" [*epithumia*] and "wish" interchangeably in his speech) – that is shared by all human agents (205a5–8). This discovery leads Socrates and Diotima to find fault with our customary usage of "love," which picks out just one species of a much more general phenomenon:

> T22: To sum up, the whole of desire for good things and for happiness is "the supreme and treacherous love", to be found in everyone; but those who direct themselves to it in all sorts of other ways, in business, or in their love of physical exercise, or in philosophy, are neither said to be "in love" nor to be "lovers", while those who proceed by giving themselves to just one kind of love have the name of the whole, "love" – and they're the ones who are "in love" and "lovers". (Plato, *Symposium* 205d1–8, trans. Rowe)

Love, conceived of as "the whole of desire for good things and for happiness," is operative in any case where an agent desires x supposing that the possession of x will make him happy. Thus the businessman, taking his happiness to consist in the accumulation of wealth, is acting under the agency of love in living a life dedicated to money-making and, properly speaking, is *in love with* money, even though we would not customarily describe him as such. Furthermore, those whom we do normally call lovers, such as Menelaus or Thrasonides, are likewise guided by the belief that their relationship with Helen or Krateia will bring them something necessary for their happiness – something good, in other words. So all cases of *erōs*, according to the customary usage of "love" as well as T22's broader conception, rely on and track the lover's beliefs about what their own happiness consists in. It is these perceived goods that *erōs* always desires to possess (cf. 205a9–b2).

Socrates addresses the cognitive foundations of *erōs* in two further ways. First, in his account of its mythological origins, Love is depicted as the offspring of Resource and Poverty (203b1–204a6) and, as a result of this dual parentage, a spirit imbued not only with motivational power but also with the cognitive resources to assess things as good and beautiful and to deliberate about how to obtain them.[92] As Frisbee Sheffield demonstrates, in characterizing Love as a "schemer after the beautiful and good" (203d3–4), Socrates' story implies a view on which *erōs* is a "deliberative desire" (2006, 46–51). Here Sheffield finds a parallel with Aristotle's notion of decision (*prohairesis*), understood as "a desire combined with thought . . . a want that emerges together with reasoning" (2006, 51). The same applies, I would add, to the Stoic "rational impulse" (*logikē hormē*, Stob. 2.87.3–5), the psychological genus of virtuous and vicious *erōs* (Section 2.4), insofar as it too is a state that marries motivation and evaluative reasoning. Second, Socrates describes the erotic pursuits of those "pregnant in body" (208e3), issuing in physical reproduction, as predicated upon the acquisition of "happiness, as they think" (208e5). Exactly what these somatic lovers take to be good, and its precise relationship with immortality, is disputed.[93] But whether it is postmortem fame or simply their own continued existence that is envisioned as good, it is clear that, for Socrates, some belief of the form "*x* is productive of my happiness" lies at the root of these erotic activities.

Crucially, for Socrates, the eudaimonistic cognition involved in *erōs* need not be correct or even phenomenologically transparent to the lover. T22's businessman, for instance, by loving wealth to the exclusion of all else and organizing his life around its sole pursuit, evinces the mistaken belief that money suffices for happiness, whether or not he has ever vocalized it. Indeed, one aim of Socratic examination more generally is to make explicit the latent views about the good that the interlocutor sincerely holds but has never previously reflected upon, so that they can be tested for consistency and soundness. And whatever else Socrates thinks about the good – it is controversial what exactly his axiological commitments are in the *Symposium* – he would surely reject as false the belief that wealth is the *sole* good. Love guided by such a belief is love done *incorrectly* (cf. 210a1). The fallibility and opacity of the eudaimonistic judgments of ordinary agents mean that love is often "treacherous" (T22), motivating the lover to acquire things that are not in fact productive of happiness on the basis of views she may not have ever consciously scrutinized.

That love is a cognitively infused motivational state, tracking the lover's eudaimonistic judgments, which can be false and opaque, is of course a central commitment of Stoic theory. As we have seen, this falls out of the Stoic identification of virtuous and vicious *erōs* as types of impulse (Section 2.4). The erotic passions of the non-wise rest on the false opinion that either sexual

---

[92] Diotima further describes Eros here as a "clever hunter" (*thēreutēs deinos*, 203d5). As we have seen, the Stoics employ the same image in their account of wise love (T3; Plutarch *Com. Not.* 1073b–c; Stob. 2.108.5–7).

[93] For insightful discussion, see Obdrzalek 2010, 420–8.

intercourse or some feature of the beloved other than virtue is good, where this cognitive cause may escape their notice (Section 2.3). The Sage, by contrast, is motivated by her evaluative knowledge to turn the beloved's talent-beauty into virtue-beauty, which is coextensive with the good (Section 3.1.3), and thus make him virtuous and a friend – that is, someone who enjoys the genuine constituents of happiness (Section 2.2). The erotic impulses of both the wise and the non-wise, then, never diverge from and are always guided by what the agent takes to be productive of happiness. Here the Stoics continue the Socratic project of explaining the nature of interpersonal love by integrating it into an intellectualist psychological framework.[94]

One potential difficulty, however, in assimilating Socrates and Diotima's erotic psychology with the Stoics' lies in the former's concern to explain the love-activity of *non-rational* creatures using the same analysis applied to human *erōs* (207a4–d2). On this view, non-rational *erōs* must involve some form of evaluative cognition in the animal, but Socrates and Diotima nowhere explain how, or whether, such cognition differs from the beliefs about the good that underlie the erotic pursuits of human agents.[95] The Stoics, for their part, leave no trace in our sources of any theory of, or interest in, non-rational *erōs*. Furthermore, their general account of the nature and scope of non-rational cognition is poorly attested and hard to reconstruct.[96] Even so, the Stoics clearly allow some form of evaluative cognition in non-rational creatures, for animals are said to perceive what is "congenial" (*oikeion*) to their constitution and to pursue it straight from birth.[97] However, cognition of the good, and any thoughts about happiness as such, are restricted to rational creatures (Seneca, *Ep.* 124.13–18). Now, Socrates and Diotima, in a correction of Aristophanes, famously deny that cognition of the *oikeion* is sufficient to motivate *erōs* (205d10–206a3). For the Stoics, however, such cognition does important work in their account of non-rational psychology. We may therefore hesitantly conjecture one of two alternatives. First, if the Stoics were minded to develop a theory of non-rational *erōs*, that theory would have to make more use of the bare cognition of the *oikeion* than Socrates and Diotima allow. Alternatively, the Stoics may have seen an inconsistency in the Socratic–Diotiman proposal: if *erōs* essentially rests on cognition of the good, but non-rational creatures cannot attain such cognition, then non-rational *erōs* is itself a confused notion.

---

94 On this Socratic project, see Sheffield 2012, 125. The Stoics stop short, however, of using "*erōs*" according to T22's broader usage, as the name for *any* cognitively infused motivation for the perceived constituents of happiness.

95 See Sheffield 2006, 53–4, and Wedgwood 2009, 305–6.

96 See Brittain 2002 and Frede 1994.

97 This claim forms the basis of the Stoic theory of *oikeiōsis*. See DL 7.85–6, Seneca, *Ep.* 121, and discussion in Klein 2016.

4.2 Against Pausanias, or Erotic Expertise without Forms

So far, I have argued for a parallel between Stoic theory and Socratic proposals in the *Symposium*, centered on the cognitive infusion of *erōs*. What of the other point of overlap I mentioned, the shared interest in erotic expertise? Before examining this second point of Stoic–Socratic contact, we must consider a rival interpretation, on which it is not Socrates but Pausanias to whom the Stoic theory of *erōs* is most directly indebted.[98] A Pausanian provenance of Stoic *erōs* has been proposed on the basis of alleged similarities in their accounts of the duality of love, the moral assessment of action, and erotic pedagogy, as well as a negative argument to the effect that the Socratic–Diotiman picture will have been anathema to the Stoics, owing to "its adamantine linkages to a transcendental metaphysics" (Inwood 1997, 58). Yet upon closer examination these similarities are difficult to sustain, for Pausanias' distinctive views are incompatible with the Stoic approach. And though there are important philosophical differences between the Stoics and the *Symposium*'s Socrates, the latter's commitment to Forms poses no obstacle to Stoic appropriation of other parts of his theory. Extracting the kernel of insight from a Platonic text and discarding the problematic ontology is in fact a typical Stoic maneuver. One upshot is the Stoic invention of erotic expertise without Forms.

I begin with Pausanias' distinction between two kinds of love. How similar is it to Stoic theory? For Pausanias, the twofold nature of Love is necessitated by the twofold nature of Aphrodite (180d3–e3): an inextricable link between *erōs* and sex is thus suggested at the beginning. Heavenly Love works with Heavenly Aphrodite, and Common Love, Common Aphrodite. The latter pair is responsible for the erotic activities of base people (*phauloi*), which are directed at both women and boys and concerned more with the body than the soul (181a8–b4), whereas Heavenly Love and Heavenly Aphrodite inspire the love of boys, beloveds who, compared to women, are "by nature stronger and more in possession of intelligence" (181c5–7). Pausanias distinguishes two forms of love, then, according to the gender of the sexual partner, and posits the existence of natural differences in the intelligence of the sexes – both clear nonstarters in the Stoa. As we have seen, the Sage's love is neither hetero- nor homoerotic, and the gender of the sexual partner plays no role whatsoever in the Stoic distinction between virtuous and vicious *erōs*; furthermore, they strenuously deny that the rational souls of men and women differ by nature, such that the former is more easily made virtuous than the latter (Section 2.2). So, even at the level of surface meaning, the Pausanian account here clashes

---

[98] See Note 88 for references.

with the Stoics'.[99] Beyond the uninformative claim that love has two forms, they could agree on little else.[100]

What about Pausanias' interest in erotic pedagogy and his views on the moral assessment of action? Regarding the latter, he asserts early in his speech that "every action is like this: when done, in and by itself it is neither fine nor shameful (*autē eph' heautēs prattomenē oute kalē oute aischra*) . . . rather the manner in which it is done is what determines how it turns out" (181a1–4). Pausanias applies this principle to both love-activity (*to eran*, 181a6–7) and the beloved's granting of sexual favors (*to charizesthai*, 183d4–8). The latter is fine, he claims, solely in the context of Heavenly Love, as a justified reward for the lover's attempts to educate the beloved in wisdom and virtue (184c7–e5), and this is so even when the lover himself *lacks* virtue, *deceives* the beloved on this score, and *fails* to improve him morally (185a5–b5). According to Pausanias, trading sex in ignorance, to a lover who feigns wisdom but cannot deliver any real ethical education, is a "fine deception" on the part of the beloved and amounts to acting "for the sake of virtue" (185b1, b5): "this is the love that belongs to the heavenly goddess," he concludes, "heavenly itself and of great value to both cities and individuals" (185b5–7).

That the best form of love is sometimes deceptive, practiced by an agent lacking virtue, with a view to stealing sex from a manipulated youth, is a proposal that would horrify the Stoics. Indeed, the emphasis Pausanias places on sex is nowhere to be found in the Stoic account of wise love. In the rare cases it transpires between Sage and beloved (Section 2.2.1), sex is never understood as a *fair trade* for imparting virtue, as if virtue were commensurable in value with sex. Lurking in Pausanias' account seems to be a crude hedonistic axiology at odds with the Stoics', not to mention an impoverished and underdeveloped account of virtue itself.

One might argue, however, that Pausanias anticipates T12's claim that "love-activity just by itself (*to eran auto monon*) is indifferent (*adiaphoron*)," and that his principle at 181a1–4 finds corroboration in the Stoic insistence that certain action-types, like speaking (cf. 181a3), are neither good nor bad.[101] Yet Socrates and Diotima also stress the intermediacy of *erōs*, positioning it between a series of ethical and epistemic poles (201e10–204c6), and in any event Pausanias' substantive account of what makes token performances of love-activity fine is

[99] Compare Inwood 1997, 57 (emphasis added): "It is Pausanias' theory, *taken at face value*, which I claim is the most appropriate backdrop for an exploration of *erōs* in Stoic thought"; ibid., 58: "it is only the *surface meaning* of the text which I suggest was relevant to the Stoic theory."

[100] On the two forms of *erōs* distinguished in Plato's *Laws*, see Reid 2019, 106–7.

[101] Inwood 1997, 56n5, 59; Nussbaum 1998, 289, 290n63. For the Stoic view, see Stob. 2.97.4 and Section 2.4.

one the Stoics could never accept. So, at most, we have here a superficial verbal echo – and an inexact one at that (cf. *autē eph' heautēs* with *auto monon*).

We are left, then, with the suggestion that Pausanias initiates Stoic interest in the "lover of good character" (183e5–6) – the erotic figure attracted to positive qualities of the soul, who forms a lifelong bond with the beloved, staying with him past the point his conventional beauty has faded (183d8–e6; cf. 182d4–6) – and in the idea that the best form of love produces friendship (183c1–4).[102] The latter claim, however, is a cultural commonplace and thus hardly unique to Pausanias.[103] And both claims could arguably be linked to Socrates himself, as he is depicted in Xenophon's *Symposium*:

> **T23**: Love of the soul is much stronger than love of the body, for we all know that no association worth speaking of is without friendship. Indeed, the loving of those who admire character is called a pleasant and willing constraint, whereas many of those who desire the body criticize and despise their beloved's way of life. Even if they love both body and soul, the ripeness of the bloom of youth is soon past its prime, and, as this goes, it is necessary that the friendship fades too, whereas the soul becomes more worthy of love (*axierastotera*) the longer it progresses toward wisdom. (Xenophon, *Symposium* 8.12–5)

Xenophon's portrait of Socrates played a key role in Zeno's early philosophical education (DL 7.2), and the depth of its influence can be gauged from the use of the term "worthy of love" (*axioerastos*) – so central in the Stoic account of wise love (T5, T14, T15) and so rare in classical and Hellenistic texts outside of Xenophon. So, when it comes to the superior endurance of love of the soul, its connection with genuine friendship, and indeed its civic benefits (Xenophon, *Symposium* 8.37–41), there is ample precedent beyond Pausanias in a Socratic text read carefully by the Stoic founder. We even find Xenophon's Socrates criticizing Pausanias by name (*Symposium* 8.32–6) and questioning the derivation of Heavenly and Common Eros from the two corresponding Aphrodites (*Symposium* 8.9–12).

So much for my response to the positive case for Pausanian influence. What of the negative argument, that Socrates' metaphysical commitments in the *Symposium* rule out any possibility of Stoic interest in his speech? The underlying premise here is dubious, for we find the Stoics closely engaging with other Platonic texts that posit Forms. The Demiurge of *Timaeus*, for instance, despite using Forms as paradigms in creating the cosmos, is seen by the Stoics as an

---

[102] Foucault 1990, 199; Nussbaum 1998, 293; Collette-Dučić 2014, 95–6.

[103] See, for example, Dover 1978, 52–3, and Aristotle, *Prior Analytics* 2.22, 68a39–68b6.

important model for their own account of the divine.[104] Far from a blanket "take it or leave it" policy, then, this example indicates that the Stoics could adopt a more nuanced interpretative response to Platonic discussions featuring Forms, endorsing and developing some proposals while rejecting the ontological framework in which they are originally embedded. No doubt this procedure sometimes leads to modifications to the Platonic proposal itself (e.g. collapsing the *Timaeus'* distinction between Demiurge and World-Soul). How, then, is Socrates and Diotima's account of erotic expertise appropriated and transformed by the Stoics?

Much of the Socratic account survives intact in Stoicism. For both, the erotic expert has perfected the evaluative cognition implicit in love by achieving *knowledge* of the nature of beauty (211d1), and on this basis lives a "life worth living" (211d1–3), that is, a happy one. Such knowledge grounds the erotic expert's "true virtue" (212a5–7). Moreover, the erotic expert is able to produce arguments that make those "decent in soul" into better people (210b7–c3). Finally, the Stoics embrace the *Lysis'* proposal that erotic expertise is partly perceptual (204b7–c2), construing it as an aspect of knowledge that allows the Sage to perceptually recognize suitable objects of love (Section 3.2.2). But the Stoics' is an erotic expertise *without Forms*, and their disagreement with Socrates and Diotima on the metaphysics of beauty generates others as well.

Both theories identify an asymmetry between the erotic expert and her beloved, but of different types altogether. For Socrates and Diotima, the erotic expert is separated by an unbridgeable metaphysical gap from the Form of Beauty she loves. The knowledge she attains of Beauty and the erotic expert herself are subject to decay (207e2–208b6), unlike the Form, which never changes or perishes (210e6–211b5). For the Stoics, however, the Sage and her beloved are metaphysically on a par – they are both changeable corporeal entities – as are the features that make them virtue- and talent-beautiful, respectively: this is just *pneuma* in various configurations. The asymmetry in Stoic wise love is thus ethical and epistemic rather than metaphysical. The Sage already possesses virtue and knowledge, and her erotic effort aims at reproducing this condition in her still vicious, but talented, beloved. By contrast, Socrates and Diotima locate perfection in the *beloved*: the Form of Beauty is beautiful without qualification and permanently existing in a way that the erotic expert could never be and will always lack. But if perfection is anywhere in the Stoic account of wise love – ethical and epistemic perfection, that is – it lies in the *lover*, and this is something of a reversal of the Socratic–Diotiman picture

---

[104] As shown by Sedley 2002, 63–5.

(204c1–6). The Sage's *erōs* is not a response to her own state of deprivation or deficiency but the beloved's.[105] This does not imply, however, that there is *no reason* for the Sage to make the beloved virtuous and a friend.[106] The Sage's self-sufficiency is compatible with her erotic efforts, which introduce new god-loved and correctly ordered beings into the cosmos, thereby serving the gods (T7).[107]

What of the *aesthetic* asymmetry between erotic expert and beloved? In rejecting the metaphysics of Forms, the Stoics must conceive of this relationship differently than Socrates and Diotima. "Pure, clean, unmixed, and not contaminated with things like human flesh, and color, and much other mortal nonsense" (211e1–3), the Form of Beauty is unconditionally beautiful, in contrast to any sensible object whose beauty is qualified in some way (cf. 211a1–5) – including the erotic expert himself. Socrates, for instance, is famously beautiful in soul but ugly in body, as Alcibiades will suggest in comparing him to a statue of Silenus (cf. 216e5–217a2). The Stoics take a different approach. Their aesthetics does not distinguish a perfect intelligible Beauty from lesser sensible beauties that only approximate it. Rather, as we saw in Section 3.1, conventional beauty, talent-beauty, and virtue-beauty are all corporeal, so that beautiful objects of any description are all equally *real*, and none is said to be more or less beautiful than another – just beautiful in different ways. Stoic beauty is therefore not so much a single "sea" (210d4) as three discrete bodies of water: the conventional, the talented, and the virtuous. The aesthetic asymmetry in Stoic wise love thus amounts to the presence of virtue-beauty in the lover alone.

One final divergence to consider is the role of pedagogy in the two theories of erotic expertise. The Stoics, of course, see ethical and epistemic education as the goal of wise love. When it comes to the *Symposium*, however, it is disputed whether the production of true virtue in others is a necessary constituent of the erotic expert's happiness.[108] Certainly the lower lovers, pregnant in soul, attempt to educate those who are "beautiful, well-born, and talented" in virtue (209a1–c2).[109] But these erotic activities are denied to flow from genuine erotic expertise; Socrates will later describe the outcome of such encounters as mere "shadow virtue" (212a4). Furthermore, in the Greater Mysteries, the moral improvement of those "decent in soul" is just one intermediate step toward

---

[105] The Sage is said to be "without lack" (*anendeēs*), whereas the non-Sage is lacking of many things (*endea . . . pollōn*) (Plutarch, *Com. Not.* 1068c; cf. Stob. 2.101.1–2).

[106] As Seneca argues in *Ep.* 9. See Collette-Dučić 2014, 104–7.

[107] On piety in Socrates' speech in the *Symposium*, see Sheffield 2017.

[108] See, for example, the exchange between Price 1997, 257–60, and Sheffield 2006, 145–7.

[109] Schofield 1991, 32, sees this passage as a "precedent" for the Stoic account of wise love.

the highest level of the ascent (210b7–c3), and it is not clear how exactly this educative activity relates to contemplation of the Form of Beauty. On the other hand, Diotima serves as Socrates' *teacher* (207c6), and she allows that one may correctly approach matters of love having been led by another (211b8–c1). It seems, then, that although there may be some role for pedagogy in Socratic–Diotiman erotic expertise, it is not conceived on the pederastic model and, in this respect, could be thought to differ from the Stoic approach.[110] Yet the Stoics do not wholeheartedly embrace that model either, as their departures from Pausanias make clear. They regard the exclusion of women from virtuous love as unjustified and reject the commensurability of sex with virtue, such that one could be traded for the other: like Socrates, the Stoics deny that wisdom is simply transferred by touch (175d3–7). At any rate, since pedagogy is not entirely absent from Socrates and Diotima's conception of erotic expertise, the Stoic response is best understood as a change in emphasis over the earlier account, rather than a wholesale repudiation of it.

5 Conclusion

To conclude this Element, I will now raise a series of philosophical objections to the Stoic theory.

First, one might object to the pedagogical character of wise *erōs*, since it presupposes, counterintuitively, that the best interpersonal relationship involves an ethical and epistemic asymmetry between lover and beloved. Isn't it rather a *partnership* between equals that should be our ideal? Here we should recall that *erōs* is not the only interpersonal relationship the Sage can adopt. Her *friendships* are indeed predicated on ethical and epistemic equality, being directed toward other Sages, and her erotic efforts are dedicated to the goal of gaining friendship. Stoic theory thus divides the labor of ideal interpersonal affairs between *erōs* and friendship – the former is a virtuous response to those who are presently deficient in knowledge, but talented, whereas the latter is the relationship she enjoys with ethical and epistemic peers. We should thus not mistake wise *erōs* as the sole mode in which the Sage relates to others, or the Stoics' final word on the best kind of interpersonal interaction.

Nonetheless, the Stoics must accept that the best *erotic* relationship is one between unequals, where one party actively strives and succeeds to improve the other. In their view, this situation is obviously superior to one in which two vicious lovers keep each other bad. But one might nevertheless suppose that, at

---

[110] Thus Collette Dučić 2014, 98–101. Socrates' rejection of the traditional pederastic model may be further witnessed in the introduction of a *female* teacher, Diotima: see Brisson 2006, Halperin 1990. That Diotima teaches Socrates erotic expertise implies that both men and women can possess it, a claim with which the Stoics agree (Section 2.2).

a conceptual level, *erōs* and pedagogy should be sharply distinguished, and that the close connection the Stoics see between them is motivated more by the influence of contemporary pederastic institutions than any principled philosophical rationale. The Stoics may reply that, if *erōs* is essentially a response to beauty, and talent is a genuine form of beauty (Section 3.1.2), then *erōs* will be linked with the effort to develop that talent to its full potential. Yet, to continue in the spirit of Plutarch's gnat objection (Section 3.1.3), this line of reasoning would also suggest that *erōs* should respond to virtue-beauty as well, which the Stoics deny, for there is no *erōs* between Sages. The suspicion remains, then, that the Stoic association of *erōs* and pedagogy is ad hoc – or, more charitably, a product of its historical context. Here the Stoics are appealing to a cultural model familiar to Hellenistic society but alien to us to contextualize the Sage's more general protreptic mission.

But if this is so, is there anything recognizably *erotic* in wise love, or is it simply a misleading label for the Sage's pedagogical activity? Plutarch charges the Stoics with terminological deception on this point: what they call "*erōs*" in the Sage is really just moral education, a process of improving the young that involves nothing answering to our intuitive concept of love (*Com. Not.* 1073c). Is Plutarch right? It depends on which intuitions about love and *erōs* we prioritize.

If love is understood as a response to beauty, requiring some kind of disinterested and non-egoistic pursuit of the beloved's good, then, yes, the Sage's *erōs* is a recognizable form of love. It is a noteworthy feature of Stoic axiology that the Sage's happiness is not made better through the addition of time (Cicero, *Fin.* 3.45–7), and every action she performs is equally good. So far as she is concerned, then, undertaking and completing an erotic effort contributes nothing to her happiness she wouldn't otherwise have. It is rather the *beloved* who, at the end of his relationship with the Sage, changes from a state of vice to virtue, experiencing genuine goods for the first time. We can infer, then, that wise *erōs* is an activity undertaken solely on behalf of the beloved: the lover's own good and happiness, being unaffected by the erotic effort, could have no role in justifying its pursuit.

Other intuitions are not so easy to reconcile with Stoic theory. If we take love to require an unconditional and permanent attachment to a concrete individual, which suffices on its own to make one's life worth living, then, no, the Sage's *erōs* is not a recognizable form of love. Gregory Vlastos famously objected to the Socratic–Diotiman account on the grounds that it misconstrues the beloved as a "placeholder of predicates" and a "complex of qualities" (1973, 26–8): what we love is the particular person before us, not an empty vessel for repeatable properties (or so the objection goes). The Stoic theory arguably falls victim to the same criticism, for it is talent-beauty – a repeatable and indeed scalar quality (Section 3) – that grounds the Sage's love. So not only is the quality that incites and sustains wise love potentially found in others but it could also be present in them to a greater degree than in one's current beloved. Perhaps the Stoics could identify some special value in an existing erotic effort, which would prevent the Sage from "trading up" for a new beloved, but I see no direct evidence of this in our sources.[111] More fundamentally, however, the Stoics deny that the presence of any concrete individual, whether virtuous or vicious, is necessary for happiness, and this is a claim that many, even those who are not romantics, will find hard to accept.[112] Wise love is not predicated on the benefits it brings to the Sage, as I argued in the preceding paragraph, but neither is it concerned that *this particular beloved* become good. Such impartiality may be welcome in a pedagogue but ghastly in a lover.

Nonetheless, the Stoic theory of *erōs* remains of significant philosophical interest. Above all, it presents a challenge to piecemeal treatments of love, which investigate the nature and value of erotic relationships in isolation from broader ethical, epistemological, aesthetic, and metaphysical theorizing. Here the Stoics carry forward the ambition of Socrates and Diotima to construct an account of erotic love that is firmly embedded within an integrated theory of human nature, the good, knowledge, beauty, and reality. As I have emphasized throughout this Element, the Stoic account of the best and worst forms of erotic love cannot be adequately appreciated without drawing on these broader tenets, a result that provides additional confirmation of the strong systematicity of Stoic philosophy. Indeed, this systematic perspective leads the Stoics to important insights into the nature of love, even if their theory cannot fully answer to all of our present-day intuitions. That our erotic pursuits are guided by our beliefs (sometimes never vocalized or made explicit) of what will make us happy, that expertise enables one to see what is genuinely worthy of love in a person, and that there is a distinctive form of beauty displayed in those with a talent for virtue are all proposals characteristic of the Stoa that may be controversial but not easily dismissed. Stoic erotics provides a window into a more expansive philosophical vista that is worthy of our continued consideration.

---

[111] Compare Schofield 1991, 35, and Graver 2007, 188–9.
[112] See, for example, the exchange between Sheffield 2012, 127–8, and Obdrzalek 2022, 223–4.

References

Arnim, J. von (1903). *Stoicorum Veterum Fragmenta*. Leipzig: Teubner. [*SVF*]

Bastianini, G. and Sedley, D. (1995). Commentarium in Platonis "Theaetetum." *Corpus dei papiri filosofici greci e latini*, 3, 227–562. [*Anonymous Commentary on the Theaetetus*]

Bett, R. (2010). Beauty and Its Relation to Goodness in Stoicism. In A. Nightingale and D. Sedley, eds., *Ancient Models of Mind*. Cambridge: Cambridge University Press, pp. 130–52.

Bobzien, S. (1998). *Determinism and Freedom in Stoic Philosophy*. Oxford: Oxford University Press.

Bobzien, S. and Shogry, S. (2020). Stoic Logic and Multiple Generality. *Philosophers' Imprint*, 20(31), 1–36.

Boys-Stones, G. (1998). Eros in Government: Zeno and the Virtuous City. *Classical Quarterly*, 48(1), 168–74.

Boys-Stones, G. (2007). Physiognomy and Ancient Psychological Theory. In S. Swain, ed., *Seeing the Face, Seeing the Soul*. Oxford: Oxford University Press, pp. 19–124.

Brennan, T. (1998). The Old Stoic Theory of Emotions. In J. Sihvola and T. Engberg-Pedersen, eds., *The Emotions in Hellenistic Philosophy*. Dordrecht: Springer, pp. 21–70.

Brennan, T. (2005). *The Stoic Life*. Oxford: Oxford University Press.

Brisson, L. (2006). Agathon, Pausanias and Diotima in Plato's *Symposium*. In J. Lesher, D. Nails, and F. Sheffield, eds., *Plato's Symposium: Issues in Interpretation and Reception*. Washington, DC: Center for Hellenic Studies, pp. 229–51.

Brittain, C. (2002). Non-Rational Perception in the Stoics and Augustine. *Oxford Studies in Ancient Philosophy*, 22, 253–308.

Čelkytė, A. (2020). *The Stoic Theory of Beauty*. Edinburgh: Edinburgh University Press.

Chadwick, H. (1980). *Origen, Contra Celsum*. Cambridge: Cambridge University Press.

Cherniss, H. (1976). *Plutarch: Moralia, Volume XIII, Part II*. Cambridge, MA: Harvard University Press.

Collette-Dučić, B. (2014). Making Friends: The Stoic Conception of Love and Its Platonic Background. In S. Stern-Gillet and G. M. Gurtler, eds., *Ancient and Medieval Concepts of Friendship*. Albany: State University of New York Press, pp. 87–116.

Cooper, J. (1999). The Unity of Virtue. In Cooper, *Reason and Emotion*. Princeton, NJ: Princeton University Press, pp. 76–117.

Cooper, J. (2005). The Emotional Life of the Wise. *The Southern Journal of Philosophy*, 43(S1), 176–218.

Dancy, J. (2017). Moral Particularism. In E. Zalta, ed., *The Stanford Encyclopedia of Philosophy*. https://plato.stanford.edu/archives/win2017/entries/moral-particularism/.

De Lacy, P. (1984). *Galen: De Placitis Hippocratis et Platonis*. Berlin: De Gruyter. [*PHP*]

Delattre, D. (2007). *Philodème de Gadara, Sur la Musique Livre IV*. Paris: Les Belles Lettres.

Dorandi, T. (2013). *Diogenes Laertius, Lives of the Eminent Philosophers*. Cambridge: Cambridge University Press. [DL]

Dover, K. (1978). *Greek Homosexuality*. London: Bloomsbury.

Foucault, M. (1990). *The History of Sexuality, Vol. 2: The Use of Pleasure*, trans. R. Hurley. London: Penguin.

Frede, M. (1994). The Stoic Conception of Reason. In K. Boudouris, ed., *Hellenistic Philosophy*. Athens: International Society for Greek Philosophy and Culture, pp. 50–63.

Frede, M. (1999). Stoic Epistemology. In K. Algra, J. Barnes, J. Mansfeld, and M. Schofield, eds., *The Cambridge History of Hellenistic Philosophy*. Cambridge: Cambridge University Press, pp. 295–322.

Furley, W. (2021). *Menander, Misoumenos or "The Hated Man."* London: Institute of Classical Studies.

Gaca, K. (2000). Early Stoic Eros. *Apeiron*, 33(3), 207–38.

Gill, C. (2006). *The Structured Self in Hellenistic and Roman Thought*. Oxford: Oxford University Press.

Gill, C. (2013). Stoic Erôs: Is There Such a Thing? In E. Sanders, C. Thumiger, and C. Carey, eds., *Erôs in Ancient Greece*. Oxford: Oxford University Press, pp. 143–58.

Glibert-Thirry, A. (1977). *Pseudo-Andronicus de Rhodes, Περὶ παθῶν*. Leiden: Brill.

Graver, M. (2002). *Cicero on the Emotions*. Chicago, IL: University of Chicago Press.

Graver, M. (2007). *Stoicism and Emotion*. Chicago, IL: University of Chicago Press.

Halperin, D. (1990). Why Is Diotima a Woman? In Halperin, *One Hundred Years of Homosexuality*. New York: Routledge, pp. 113–51.

Hense, O. (1905). *C. Musonii Rufi Reliquiae*. Leipzig: Teubner.

Ierodiakonou, K. (2022). Intuitions in Stoic Philosophy. *British Journal for the History of Philosophy*, 31(4), 614–29.

Inwood, B. (1985). *Ethics and Human Action in Early Stoicism*. Oxford: Oxford University Press.

Inwood, B. (1997). Why Do Fools Fall in Love? In R. Sorabji, ed., *Aristotle and After*. London: Institute of Classical Studies, pp. 55–69.

Inwood, B. (2007). *Seneca, Selected Philosophical Letters*. Oxford: Oxford University Press.

Inwood, B. and Gerson, L. (1997). *Hellenistic Philosophy: Introductory Readings, Second Edition*. Indianapolis, IN: Hackett.

Irwin, T. (1995). *Plato's Ethics*. Oxford: Oxford University Press.

Klein, J. (2016). The Stoic Argument from *oikeiōsis*. *Oxford Studies in Ancient Philosophy*, 50, 143–200.

Klein, J. (2021). Desire and Impulse in Epictetus and the Older Stoics. *Archiv für Geschichte der Philosophie*, 103(2), 221–51.

Konstan, D. and Ramelli, I. (2009). *Hierocles the Stoic: Elements of Ethics, Fragments and Excerpts*. Atlanta, GA: Society of Biblical Literature.

Laurand, V. (2007). L'érôs pédagogique chez Platon et les stoïciens. In M. Bonazzi and C. Helmig, eds., *Platonic Stoicism, Stoic Platonism*. Leuven: Leuven University Press, pp. 63–86.

Long, A. and Sedley, D. (1987). *The Hellenistic Philosophers*. 2 vols. Cambridge: Cambridge University Press.

Marcovich, M. (2002). *Clementis Alexandrini Paedagogus*. Leiden: Brill.

Nussbaum, M. (1994). *The Therapy of Desire*. Princeton, NJ: Princeton University Press.

Nussbaum, M. (1998). Eros and the Wise: The Stoic Response to a Cultural Dilemma. In J. Sihvola and T. Engberg-Pedersen, eds., *The Emotions in Hellenistic Philosophy*. Dordrecht: Springer, pp. 271–304.

Obdrzalek, S. (2010). Moral Transformation and the Love of Beauty in Plato's *Symposium*. *Journal of the History of Philosophy*, 48(4), 415–44.

Obdrzalek, S. (2022). Why *Erōs*? In D. Ebrey and R. Kraut, eds., *The Cambridge Companion to Plato*, 2nd ed. Cambridge: Cambridge University Press, pp. 202–32.

Price, A. (1997). *Love and Friendship in Plato and Aristotle*. Reprinted with Afterword. Oxford: Oxford University Press.

Price, A. (2002). Plato, Zeno, and the Object of Love. In M. Nussbaum and J. Sihvola, eds., *The Sleep of Reason*. Chicago, IL: University of Chicago Press, pp. 170–99.

Reid, J. (2019). Plato on Love and Sex. In A. Martin, ed., *The Routledge Handbook of Love in Philosophy*. New York: Routledge, pp. 105–15.

Reinhardt, T. (2019). *Pithana* and *Probabilia*. In T. Bénatouïl and K. Ierodiakonou, eds., *Dialectic after Plato and Aristotle*. Cambridge: Cambridge University Press, pp. 218–53.

Reydams-Schils, G. (2005). *The Roman Stoics*. Chicago, IL: University of Chicago Press.

Rowe, C. (1998). *Plato, Symposium: Edited with an Introduction, Translation and Commentary*. Oxford: Aris & Phillips.

Rowe, C. (2006). The *Symposium* as a Socratic Dialogue. In J. Lesher, D. Nails, and F. Sheffield, eds., *Plato's Symposium: Issues in Interpretation and Reception*. Washington, DC: Center for Hellenic Studies, pp. 9–22.

Schofield, M. (1984). Ariston of Chios and the Unity of Virtue. *Ancient Philosophy*, 4(1), 83–96.

Schofield, M. (1991). *The Stoic Idea of the City*. Cambridge: Cambridge University Press.

Sedley, D. (2002). The Origins of Stoic God. In D. Frede and A. Laks, eds., *Traditions of Theology*. Leiden: Brill, pp. 41–83.

Sheffield, F. (2006). *Plato's Symposium: The Ethics of Desire*. Oxford: Oxford University Press.

Sheffield, F. (2012). The *Symposium* and Platonic Ethics: Plato, Vlastos, and a Misguided Debate. *Phronesis*, 57(2), 117–41.

Sheffield, F. (2017). Platonic Piety: Putting Humpty Dumpty Together Again. In A. Petersen and G. van Kooten, eds., *Religio-philosophical Discourses in the Mediterranean World*. Leiden: Brill, pp. 37–62.

Shogry, S. (2021). Psychological Disease and Action-Guiding Impressions in Early Stoicism. *British Journal for the History of Philosophy*, 29(5), 784–805.

Shogry, S. (2022). The Starting-Points for Knowledge. *Phronesis*, 67(1), 62–98.

Shogry, S. (in press). Seneca on Moral Improvement through Dialectical Study: A Chrysippean Reading of *Letter* 87. *Ancient Philosophy*.

Srinivasan, A. (2020). Sex as a Pedagogical Failure. *Yale Law Journal*, 129(4), 1100–46.

Stephens, W. (1996). Epictetus on How the Stoic Sage Loves. *Oxford Studies in Ancient Philosophy*, 14, 193–210.

Taylor, C. (1982). The End of the *Euthyphro*. *Phronesis*, 27(2), 109–18.

Tieleman, T. (2003). *Chrysippus' On Affections*. Leiden: Brill.

Visnjic, J. (2021). *The Invention of Duty*. Leiden: Brill.

Vlastos, G. (1973). The Individual as Object of Love in Plato. In Vlastos, *Platonic Studies*. Princeton, NJ: Princeton University Press, pp. 3–34.

Vogt, K. (2008). *Law, Reason, and the Cosmic City*. Oxford: Oxford University Press.

Wachsmuth, C. (1884). *Ioannis Stobaei Anthologii*. Berlin: Weidmann. [Stob.]

Walsh, P. (1998). *Cicero: The Nature of the Gods*. Oxford: Oxford University Press.

Wedgwood, R. (2009). Diotima's Eudaemonism. *Phronesis*, 54(4–5), 297–325.

Acknowledgments

For constructive feedback on earlier versions of this material, I am grateful to audiences at Princeton, Cambridge, the Oxford Philological Society, and the Pacific APA. For helpful discussion and correspondence, I warmly thank Suzanne Obdrzalek, Ralph Wedgwood, Frisbee Sheffield, Malcolm Schofield, Tamer Nawar, David Sedley, Gábor Betegh, Harold Tarrant, Nick Denyer, John Sellars, Gregory Hutchinson, Guy Westwood, Sophie Bocksberger, Aneurin Ellis-Evans, Arnaud Petit, Janine Gühler, Stefan Sienkiewicz, Luca Castagnoli, Alesia Preite, Hermann Koerner, Alexander Prescott-Couch, Rachel Achs, Marion Durand, Allison Piñeros Glasscock, and Alexander Bown. I am particularly indebted to Jeremy Reid, Edward Platts, Anthony Price, James Warren, and an anonymous referee for reading through the whole draft and offering many suggestions and objections that improved the final product. All errors and shortcomings are my own.

Cambridge Elements ☰

Ancient Philosophy

James Warren
University of Cambridge

James Warren is Professor of Ancient Philosophy at the University of Cambridge. He is the author of *Epicurus and Democritean Ethics* (Cambridge, 2002), *Facing Death: Epicurus and his Critics* (2004), *Presocratics* (2007) and *The Pleasures of Reason in Plato, Aristotle and the Hellenistic Hedonists* (Cambridge, 2014). He is also the editor of *The Cambridge Companion to Epicurus* (Cambridge, 2009), and joint editor of *Authors and Authorities in Ancient Philosophy* (Cambridge, 2018).

About the Series

The Elements in Ancient Philosophy series deals with a wide variety of topics and texts in ancient Greek and Roman philosophy, written by leading scholars in the field. Taking a theme, question, or type of argument, some Elements explore it across antiquity and beyond. Others look in detail at an ancient author, a specific work, or a part of a longer work, considering its structure, content, and significance, or explore more directly ancient perspectives on modern philosophical questions.

Cambridge Elements ≡

Ancient Philosophy

Elements in the Series

Relative Change
Matthew Duncombe

Plato's Ion: *Poetry, Expertise, and Inspiration*
Franco V. Trivigno

Aristotle on Ontological Priority in the Categories
Ana Laura Edelhoff

The Method of Hypothesis and the Nature of Soul in Plato's Phaedo
John Palmer

Aristotle on Women: Physiology, Psychology, and Politics
Sophia M. Connell

The Hedonism of Eudoxus of Cnidus
Richard Davies

Properties in Ancient Metaphysics
Anna Marmodoro

Vice in Ancient Philosophy
Karen Margrethe Nielsen

Stoic Eros
Simon Shogry

A full series listing is available at: www.cambridge.org/EIAP

Printed in the United States
by Baker & Taylor Publisher Services